VHDL BY EXAMPLE

A Concise Introduction for FPGA Design

VHDL BY EXAMPLE

A Concise Introduction for FPGA Design

Blaine C. Readler

Full Arc
Press

VHDL BY EXAMPLE
A Concise Introduction for FPGA Design

Published by Full Arc Press

Visit us at: http://www.readler.com

E-mail: blaine@readler.com

An acknowledgement and thanks to Lulu Enterprises, Inc. for making the publishing of this book possible.

http://www.lulu.com

ISBN: 978-0-9834973-5-6

Printed in the United States of America

First Edition: 2014

Dedicated to the memory of Steve Byars, who provided an exemplary model in both engineering and being human. The man is gone, but the examples to which we aspire live on.

Contents

Introduction

This book is a close cousin of the previously published Verilog by Example. It was two years in coming because I have been busy using the subject matter to pay my bills. As with the previous FPGA language reference, this too has the goal to have you looking at workable examples by the shortest path possible. Like any descriptive language, whether verilog, VHDL, or C++, there are layers of features and capabilities that will ultimately be brought to bear if you use it long enough, but most of which can represent just a confusing distraction if introduced early on. This book initially strips away all but the very bare essentials to show you those fundamental aspects of the language that are universally required in almost any design. Later, it builds, feature-by-feature, more sophisticated capabilities.

The material is intended for students and engineers, both hardware and software, who already have a working knowledge of digital design and operation. It is not an instructional text on how to design logic. Additionally, it is intended to provide a very quick entry into VHDL basics; it is not a comprehensive reference. But I'm sure you didn't expect that for less than $20.

The contexts of the examples assume FPGAs (versus ASICs or, God forbid, discrete logic). This is by far the most ubiquitous use of HDL (Hardware Description Language) today. And in any case, if you're just learning HDL, it is highly unlikely that you've been hired to do ASIC development.

All examples used in this book are available as text files at:

http://www.readler.com

A note about punctuation: commas and periods are generally placed before closing parenthesis. For example, the following words might describe my approach to writing this book: "fastidious," "thorough," and "clarity." However, I have taken the liberty to break this rule throughout the following text in order to avoid confusion about the exact spelling of signal names. So, for example, in this context I might write that "in_1", "out_1", and "enable_b" comprise all the signals of block "mux_2".

The Tool Flow

This subject could be a whole book onto itself, but I will limit it here to just what's needed to see how VHDL code is used. VHDL, like verilog, is a hardware description language (HDL), and as such, completely describes how the logic design works. Along with a device-specific file defining implementation details such as device package type, I/O pin assignments, etc., the VHDL code is all that's needed to create an operating FPGA. The "operating FPGA" is embodied in a binary object file that is loaded into the device after power-up. The tools described here are used to get from the VHDL source code to this loadable binary object file.

Step 1: coding

This is simply the process of laying the ideas in your head down into VHDL code, which is just a text file. If you've done software coding, you are completely familiar with this step. Any text editor will work, but professional text editors will help by color-coding syntax categories of VHDL (assuming your version supports VHDL);

Step 2: simulation

Although not strictly necessary to achieve a successfully compiled load file, simulation should be considered a practical requirement. Foregoing this step would be like spending months designing, building, and packing a parachute, and then jumping out of a plane without ever testing it. There is a finite possibility your design will work as intended—decreasing rapidly with complexity—but more than likely you will see the ground rushing up at you as you engage power and your FPGA does absolutely nothing.

Step 3: synthesis

The first two steps were your creative contribution. Step 3 begins the automated process of translating your text into operating logic. The synthesis step can be thought of as a bridge between your human text description and a gate-level representation. Gate-level here doesn't necessarily mean just AND and OR gates, but includes basic functional blocks as muxes and flip-flops. It is at this step that we find out if our code can be practically translated into logic that can be implemented in an FPGA. The output from the synthesis step looks very much like a netlist. Expensive stand-alone synthesis tools are often used for large or complex designs, but most FPGA vendor software includes synthesis that is quite adequate for many applications.

Step 4: compile

Whereas the synthesis of step 3 still comprises somewhat abstract logic constructs, the final compile step maps the synthesis netlist-like logic description into the specific logic and routing resources of the FPGA device. This step is always performed by the vendor software. We can define pins assignments, or let the tool automatically assign them (almost never done on all but the most difficult designs). It is in this compile step that we find out if the design that was synthesizable can actually be implemented into our chosen device. The output of the compile step is the binary load file that is used to configure the FPGA.

In and Out

First a word about coding style is necessary. What you find in this book are the author's methods developed over many years of practice. The goal should always be to produce readable code that is easy to understand. Different people have different preferences, though, and you will find as many individual styles as there are people coding. About the only absolutely wrong style is no style, i.e., where all the text is smashed to the left margin with no indenting or consistent parenthetical grouping. You should note that there are many shortcuts that could be taken with the code used throughout this book, but you'll never be wrong by including optional parenthesis or white spaces, but you could very well cause your code to synthesize in an unintended manner if you make careless eliminations.

The synthesis tool expects certain standard file structures. We'll start with almost the simplest design possible in order to introduce the minimum requirements: two combinatorial operations on three inputs. Here's how it looks as logic block flow. Note that this box represents the entire FPGA.

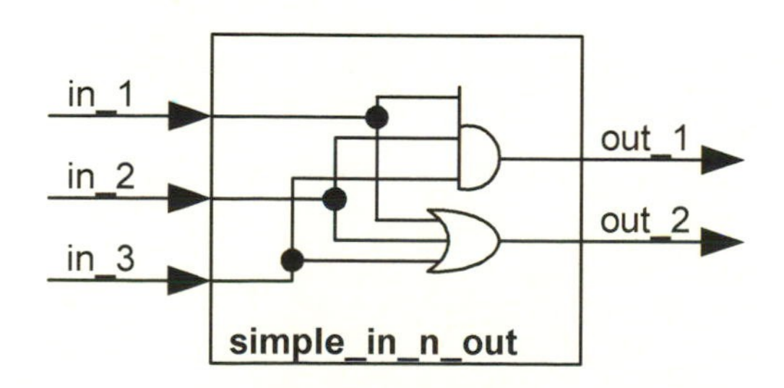

Simple In and Out

The VHDL code can be seen on the next page. The text file implements one module or "entity", which for this simple design is the entire design. The word "entity" is a required keyword, and is followed by the name of the entity. For our purposes, an entity is always synonymous with a file, so the entity name is the same as the file name. Note, though, that the entity name has no file extension (which for VHDL is always "vhd", e.g., "simple_in_n_out.vhd").

```
-- ------------------------------------------------
-- Header information -- details about the context,
-- constraints, etc..
-- ------------------------------------------------
library IEEE;
use IEEE.STD_LOGIC_1164.all;

entity simple_in_n_out is
  port (
         -- Inputs
         in_1   : in  std_logic;
         in_2   : in  std_logic;
         in_3   : in  std_logic;
         -- Outputs
         out_1  : out std_logic;
         out_2  : out std_logic
       );
end entity simple_in_n_out;

architecture simple_in_n_out_arch of simple_in_n_out is

begin

    -- ------------ Design implementation --------

    out_1 <= in_1 AND in_2 AND in_3;
    out_2 <= in_1 OR  in_2 OR  in_3;

end architecture simple_in_n_out_arch;
```

Simple In and Out

Notice that we've skipped over two lines, the first starting with "library." For the sake of keeping things initially simple, we're going to ignore these for the moment, but for now know that library declarations will be included in every design.

A port list follows the name of the entity, beginning with the word "port" and demarked by parenthesis. Each port of the entity is a signal (or group of signals) that enters (inputs) or leaves (outputs) the design. The ports are separated by semi-colons. Note that the last port in the list has no semi-colon. Each port entry consists of the port (i.e., signal) name, followed by a colon, followed by the direction, and ending with a declaration of the signal type. So the name of the first port is "in_1", and the signal type is "std_logic", which stands for "standard logic" and is the most common type of signal. Note that this example groups all the inputs first, but this is not required—inputs and outputs can occur in any order.

Following the port list is the line that marks the end of the entity declaration. Note that it ends with a semi-colon.

The entity declaration simply establishes the ports (the inputs and outputs) of the module. The actual implementation of the design, the description of the functionality, follows in the next and last section called the "architecture". VHDL allows multiple architectures to be associated with one entity, but for our purposes here, and for the rest of the book, and indeed for most of the designs you may ever do, there will be one architecture for each entity.

The architecture is declared using a name, here called "simple_in_n_out_arch". The name could be anything, "duck" for example. The "of simple_in_n_out" is not arbitrary, however. The architecture has to be "of" the entity. This may seem redundant, since the entity is right there above, but VHDL allows an architecture (multiple architectures) to be located in a different file. This is something we will never do in this book.

This is a good time to note that VHDL allows levels of complexity that are not needed in simple designs, and in fact often not even in moderate to large designs as well. The extended complexities possible with VHDL are useful in situations of greater sophistication, such as mixed language development and simulation (VHDL and C++, for example), and team-oriented projects such as large ASICs. I will note areas where greater complexity could be introduced so that you can get a feel for the full scope of the language, but be assured that the material covered in this book will suffice for all your needs, unless you become a career FPGA/ASIC developer, in which case, you'll obviously be taking studies beyond this introduction. But even then, everything you learn here will still apply in the larger scope.

Back to the example, the architecture declaration is followed by the keyword "begin", and then the design itself finally does begin.

The design description for the simple logic shown above consists of just two lines of combinatorial assignment code (also called continuous assignments). Logical operations in VHDL are denoted conveniently with the selfsame words. Note that the operation assignments are "<=", not just the equal sign as in some software programming languages.

Double dashes indicate a comment, and the synthesis software ignores everything that follows to the end of the line. Thus, the entire line containing "Design implementation" is just a comment.

The end of the architecture section (and also the text file here) is marked by the keywords "end architecture", followed by the name of the architecture.

A word about font case: VHDL is not case sensitive, so the synthesis software will recognize "out_1" as the same as "Out_1" as the same as "OUT_1". I see no reason for mixing cases among multiple instances of the same label other than for purposeful confusion. Note that I've used upper case for the logical operators "AND" and "OR"; I could have used lower case, but this helps to visually differentiate them from the operands.

The simple In and Out design just described defines outputs that are direct logical operations of inputs only. Virtually all practical designs, though, will have internal signals. In VHDL these are called, reasonably, "signals". As we will see later, signals can be the outputs of registers, or used to inter-connected lower-level hierarchical modules, but here we see how a signal can be an intermediate stage of combinatorial processing.

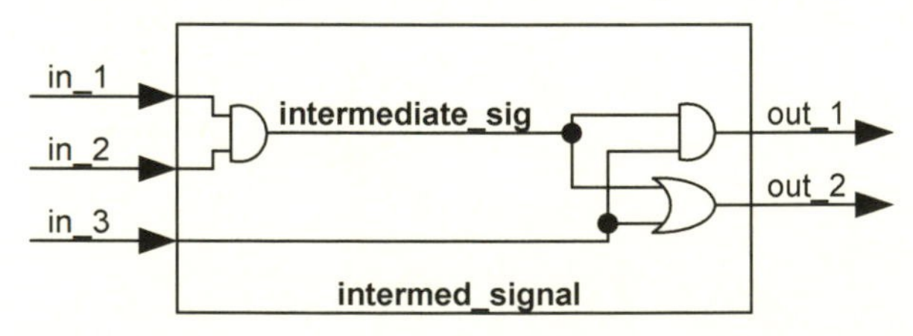

Intermediate Signal

Signals must be declared, and this occurs between the beginning of the architecture declaration and the keyword "begin" (this is where all the declarations for the architecture are made). The word "signal" is the keyword, followed by the signal name. The colon is required and is always followed by the type of signal (again std_logic). As with all VHDL endings, a semi-colon closes out the line.

In the body of the architecture that follows, the intermediate signal is assigned the logical operation "in_1 AND in_2" in exactly the same manner that we've already assigned logical operations to the entity outputs. Note that we've introduced a comment at the end of the assignment line.

```
-- ------------------------------------------------
-- Header information
-- ------------------------------------------------
library IEEE;
use IEEE.STD_LOGIC_1164.all;

entity intermed_signal is
  port (
         -- Inputs
         in_1   : in  std_logic;
         in_2   : in  std_logic;
         in_3   : in  std_logic;
         -- Outputs
         out_1  : out std_logic;
         out_2  : out std_logic
       );
end entity intermed_signal;

architecture intermed_signal_arch of intermed_signal is

   signal intermediate_sig : std_logic;

begin
    -- ------------- Design implementation --------

    intermediate_sig <= in_1 AND in_2; --intermediate sig.

    out_1 <= intermediate_sig AND in_3;
    out_2 <= intermediate_sig OR  in_3;

end architecture intermed_signal_arch;
```

Intermediate Signal

Now that you're becoming comfortable with the overall structure of an entity and associated architecture, we'll back up and explain the library declarations at the beginning of the files. It is not an exaggeration to say that the real meat of VHDL is contained in libraries. In a way, the VHDL language itself is just a shell within which we use libraries to build both the simple and complex operators that we associate with high level languages in general. Designers can even create their own libraries, but that is beyond the scope of this book. Rather, we will use standard libraries codified by the IEEE organization. These libraries are universal, and recognized by every development tool. We will introduce different IEEE libraries as the needs arise, but STD_LOGIC_1164 provides the fundamental definitions to implement our very simple introductory examples, including the ubiquitous "std_logic" type signal, along with the core logic operators (AND, OR, etc.). Think of std_logic signals as wires communicating logic ones and zeros.

Logic designs often (usually) include multi-bit buses. These are represented in VHDL as vector signals, and the width is defined as part of the declaration. Single-bit signals are called scalars. The following example performs a combinatorial operation on two 4-bit input buses (AKA vectors) and a single-bit (AKA scalar) control signal.

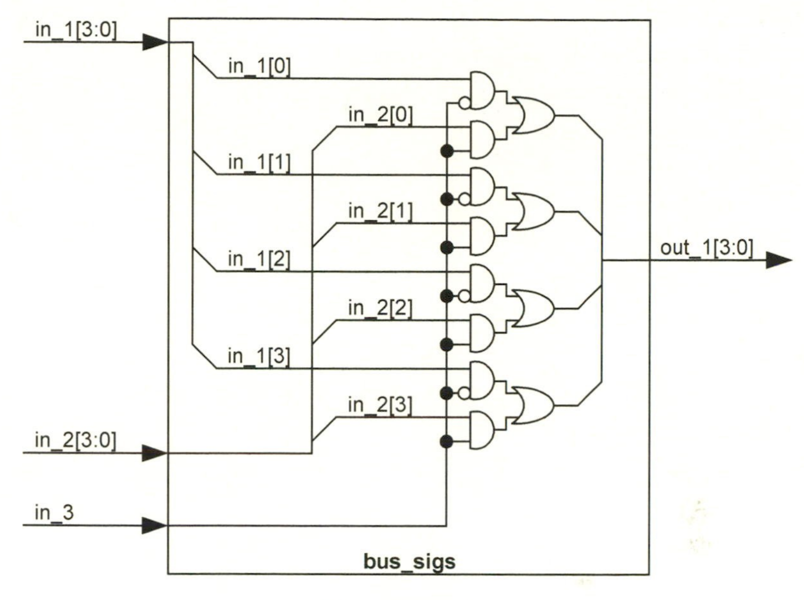

Bus Signals

Essentially, when “in_3” is low, then “in_1” is selected, and when “in_3” is high, “in_2” is selected. This is of course a two-input bus multiplexer.

Comparing the block flow diagram with the code on the following page, we can see that VHDL vector representation of buses provides for compact representation (the logic for a whole bus is contained in one line). We note that the original “std_logic” type signals are replaced with “std_logic_vector(3 downto 0)” for those signals that have become buses (AKA vectors). The “(3 downto 0)” stands in for the more familiar “[3:0]”, and is one example of why many consider VHDL more verbose over verilog.

We also see a mysterious intermediate “in_3_bus” signal. This is due to the manner of logical operation of the “AND” and “OR” operators. These perform bitwise operations, and expect the two values to be of equal bus size. Thus, the first assign statement extends the single-bit “in_3” to a 4-bit “in_3_bus”, whereby all the bits of the new bus have the same value as the original “in_3”. This is done using the concatenation operator “&” (not to be confused with the logical AND), which is used to pull together individual bit signals into vectors. Note that the bit signal on the left is the MSB.

Note that "NOT" is a bitwise negation operator, i.e., it inverts each bit of the vector signal (bus "in_3_bus").

```
-- ------------------------------------------------
-- Header information
-- ------------------------------------------------
library IEEE;
use IEEE.STD_LOGIC_1164.all;

entity bus_sigs is
  port (
         -- Inputs
         in_1    : in  std_logic_vector(3 downto 0);
         in_2    : in  std_logic_vector(3 downto 0);
         in_3    : in  std_logic;
         -- Outputs
         out_1   : out std_logic_vector(3 downto 0)
       );
end entity bus_sigs;

architecture bus_sigs_arch of bus_sigs is

   signal in_3_bus  : std_logic_vector(3 downto 0);

begin
    ----------- Design implementation --------

    in_3_bus <= (in_3 & in_3 & in_3 & in_3);

    out_1 <=     ( (NOT in_3_bus) AND in_1)
             OR (in_3_bus AND in_2);

end architecture bus_sigs_arch;
```

Bus Signals

The next block logic diagram shows the logic gates of the previous diagram collected together into a standard mux symbol. Note that we have not changed the function, just the representation.

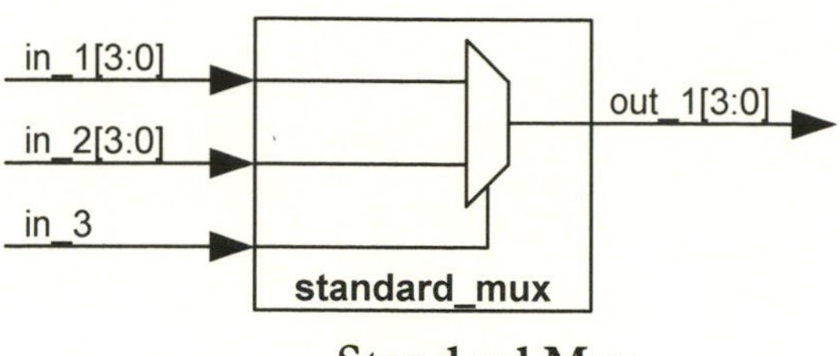

Standard Mux

The standard_mux_1.vhd VHDL code on the next page, although also functionally equivalent to the previous code, now reflects a different and more compact way of representing the multiplexer function. We here introduce VHDL's first (of two) combinatorial conditional constructs, eliminating the "in_3_bus" intermediate signal of the previous example in the process. The assign statement reads as such: "select in_1 for out_1 when signal in_3_bus (the select control) is 0, else select in_2 for out_1 when signal in_3_bus is 1, else select all-zeroes for everything else". The selection condition inside the parenthesis (which are optional—I include them for clarity) can be a complete expression, e.g., (a AND (b or (NOT c))).

You may be wondering why I included the last "cover everything else" selection condition, and your query would be justified since the first two selections would seem to already cover all possible combinations (0 and 1). The unobvious reality is that the std_logic library includes other states besides just 0 and 1 (e.g., 'z' for high impedance). The bottom line is that you should just always include a last "others" condition, needed or not, otherwise the simulation and synthesis tools will bark.

Notice that logic 0's and 1's include single quotation marks; this is how we indicate std_logic zero and one states. On the other hand, std_logic_vector's form is to include double quotation marks, thus, the "0000" indicates what we might be more familiar with as 0x0.

```
-- ------------------------------------------------
-- Header information
-- ------------------------------------------------
library IEEE;
use IEEE.STD_LOGIC_1164.all;

entity standard_mux_1 is
  port (
         -- Inputs
         in_1   : in  std_logic_vector(3 downto 0);
         in_2   : in  std_logic_vector(3 downto 0);
         in_3   : in  std_logic;
         -- Outputs
         out_1  : out std_logic_vector(3 downto 0)
       );
end entity standard_mux_1;

architecture standard_mux_1_arch of standard_mux_1 is

begin

   with (in_3) select
      out_1 <=  in_1 when '0',
                in_2 when '1',
              "0000" when others;

end architecture standard_mux_1_arch;
```

Standard Mux 1

The second VHDL combinatorial conditional construct is shown in the standard_mux_2.vhd code example. Where the previous method was "select with", this one is "when, else". The operation here reads: "when in_3_bus (the select control) is low, use in_1, else use in_2." This works very much like a limited version of the familiar IF/THEN statement of other languages.

Note that although a single instance of this conditional selection statement is used here, these can be concatenated. Here's an example:

```
final_value <= input_1 when (select_1 = '1') else
               input_2 when (select_2 = '1') else
               input_3 when (select_3 = '1') else
               default_val;
```

Again, the parenthesis are optional. Note that in this case a final default value must be included, otherwise the synthesis software will implement a (presumably unintended) latch.

```
-- ------------------------------------------------------
-- Header information
-- ------------------------------------------------------
library IEEE;
use IEEE.STD_LOGIC_1164.all;

entity standard_mux_2 is
  port (
         -- Inputs
         in_1    : in  std_logic_vector(3 downto 0);
         in_2    : in  std_logic_vector(3 downto 0);
         in_3    : in  std_logic;
         -- Outputs
         out_1   : out std_logic_vector(3 downto 0)
       );
end entity standard_mux_2;

architecture standard_mux_2_arch of standard_mux_2 is

begin

   out_1 <= in_1 when (in_3 = '0') else in_2;

end architecture standard_mux_2_arch;
```

Standard Mux 2

Finally, before we move beyond strictly combinatorial operation, we'll explore a few more details associated with buses. Where in the previous examples we selected entire buses for the output, here we break the buses out and then recombine them after some processing. Note that both input buses are four bits, but the output bus is six bits.

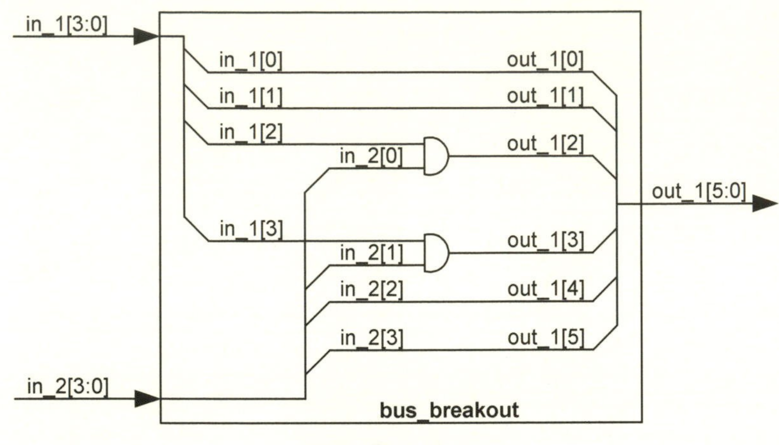

Bus Breakout

All of the combinatorial and bus reconstruction shown in the module above is implemented in one assignment in the code on the opposite page. Here we introduce an expansion of the concatenation operator "&". I have arranged the concatenation elements vertically on separate lines for clarity, but they could all be included on the same (albeit long) line, still separated by "&". Note again that the MS element is always first (i.e., next to the left-most parenthesis), while the LS element is always last (next to the right-most parenthesis). The parenthesis are not necessary, and are included for clarity. Notice that the first and last elements here comprise two bits, and that the two middle elements (each one bit) are the result of combinatorial operations.

```
-- ------------------------------------------------
-- Header information
-- ------------------------------------------------
library IEEE;
use IEEE.STD_LOGIC_1164.all;

entity bus_breakout is
  port (
        -- Inputs
        in_1   : in  std_logic_vector(3 downto 0);
        in_2   : in  std_logic_vector(3 downto 0);
        in_3   : in  std_logic;
        -- Outputs
        out_1  : out std_logic_vector(5 downto 0)
      );
end entity bus_breakout;

architecture bus_breakout_arch of bus_breakout is

begin
    --------------- Design implementation --------

    out_1 <= (   in_2(3 downto 2)
               & (in_1(3) AND in_2(1))
               & (in_1(2) AND in_2(0))
               & in_1(1 downto 0)
             );

end architecture bus_breakout_arch;
```

Bus Breakout

Clocks and Registers

In the introduction, I indicated that this book assumes that you have a working familiarity with digital design. The rubber is about to meet the road.

Clocked state logic comprises the vast majority of the workings of modern FPGAs, and it is here that the true complexity and sophistication of any hardware descriptive language unfolds. The fundamental principles of clocked operation in VHDL, though, are straightforward, and easy to grasp if we take them a step at a time.

Until now, our code has consisted of continuous assignments, i.e., direct combinatorial logic. These statements are continuous in the sense that the output signal (the one being assigned) is continuously responsive to any and all inputs. Any input that changes (and is not gated off by the intervening logic) will immediately affect the output (ignoring physical delays). Contrary to this, registers hold or store information, and therefore require a different coding mechanism called a process statement. While process statements can be used for other logic besides strictly clocked registers, for us for now, a process statement means a clocked register.

We'll begin by implementing the simplest form of a D-flop. Since this represents the basis for the various forms of registers we will continue to encounter, it is labeled as a "Reg." As shown in the timing diagram, output "out_1" follows "input in_1" at the clocked edges.

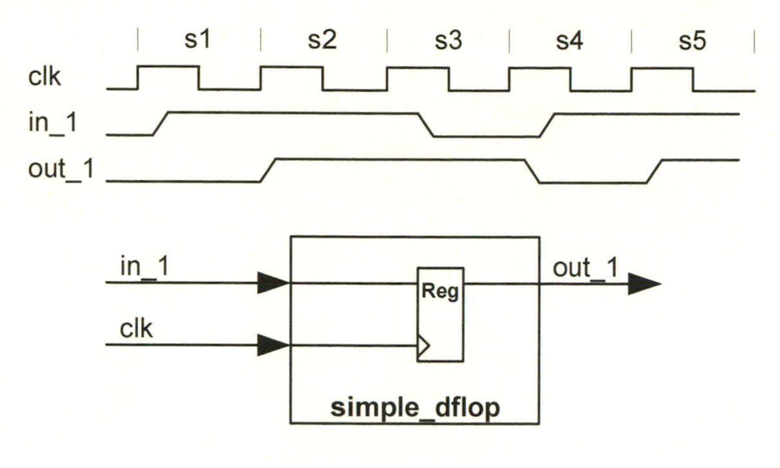

Simple D-flop

The process statement that here comprises the entire contents of the architecture body implements the simple one-bit register shown above. Process statements always start with a label, here indicated as “Reg_Proc”. Again, “duck” would have sufficed. The colon and the keyword “process” are required, as are the parenthesis and the contents therein. The parenthesis contain what is called the sensitivity list, and this process statement is only executed when something in the sensitivity list changes. Since the only sensitivity signal in this process statement is the clock signal, the output “out_1” will only change at clock edges, thus a clocked register.

But we haven’t yet defined which clock edge, rising or falling, to allow the output to change. That definition follows in the body of the process statement with the conditional “if rising_edge(clk)”. Process statements can include general if/then conditional constructs (as well as case statements, for-loops, etc. as we’ll see later), but “rising_edge” has a specific meaning, and indicates to the synthesis tool that this process is actually registered signals (technically, “rising_edge” is not a built-in part of VHDL, but a defined function in the IEEE.STD_LOGIC_1164 library). If we happened to want a falling-edge register, the IF condition would be, not surprisingly, “if falling_edge(clk)”. Note that “clk” inside the parenthesis is not a keyword, but rather the name we’ve given to our clock signal. The "begin" and "end process;" wording are required, and included in every process statement.

A side note: another method of defining registers, one that is falling out of practice, would be "if (clk'event AND clk = 1)", and "if (clk'event AND clk = 0)", respectively. I include these in case you should happen upon them.

The operation is easy to see: at every rising clock edge (and only at a rising clock edge), the value of "in_1" is assigned to "out_1".

```
-- -----------------------------------------------
-- Header information
-- -----------------------------------------------
library IEEE;
use IEEE.STD_LOGIC_1164.all;

entity simple_dflop is
  port (
         -- Inputs
         clk    : in  std_logic;
         in_1   : in  std_logic;
         -- Outputs
         out_1  : out std_logic
       );
end entity simple_dflop;

architecture simple_dflop_arch of simple_dflop is

begin
    --------------- Design implementation --------

   Reg_Proc: process (clk)
   begin
      if rising_edge(clk) then
         out_1 <= in_1;
      end if;
   end process;

end architecture simple_dflop_arch;
```

Simple D-flop

Next we add an asynchronous reset to our simple D-flop. The timing diagram shows the operation where "reset" forces "out_1" low immediately during state s3, and "out_1" then remains low until clocked again back high at state s5.

My convention will be that asynchronous controls (resets and presets) will enter the register box at the top or bottom, while all synchronous controls will connect to the front.

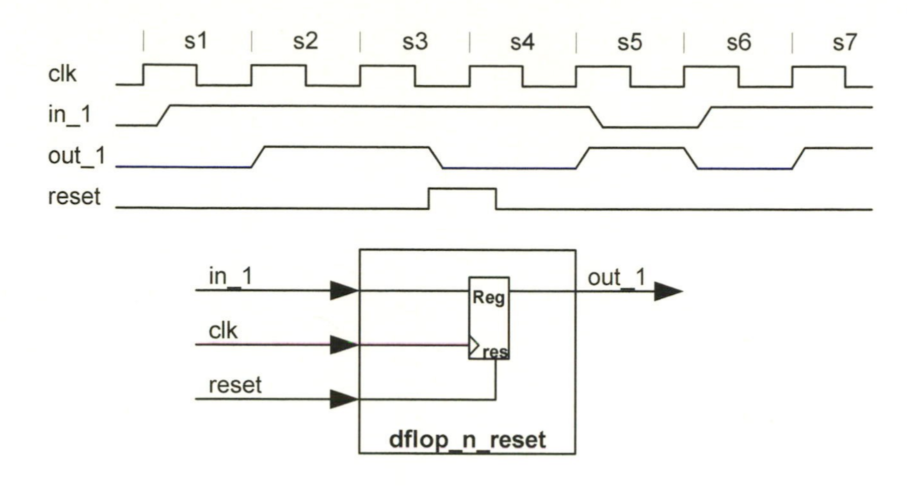

D-flop with reset

In the code on the next page you can see that the process statement has now grown to accommodate the reset. Since the reset is asynchronous and results in activity immediately, it must be included in the sensitivity list. The body of the process has now become more complicated as we introduce if/else conditional statements to accommodate the reset. Any time "reset" is one, "out_1" is forced to zero. Since this happens as soon as reset goes active (reset is part of the sensitivity list) you can see that this effects an asynchronous clear. When reset is not high, then the "else" original in-to-out register assignment is selected (occurring only at rising clock edges).

Asynchronous controls must always precede the "elsif rising_edge(clk)" clocked assignments. Otherwise, since if/elsif/else conditional statements are sequence prioritized (meaning that once a condition is met, the subsequent tests are skipped), the reset would be overridden at each clock edge, and this would contradict what we want with an asynchronous clear.

```
-- -------------------------------------------------------
-- Header information
-- -------------------------------------------------------
library IEEE;
use IEEE.STD_LOGIC_1164.all;

entity dflop_n_reset is
  port (
         -- Inputs
         clk    : in  std_logic;
         reset  : in  std_logic;
         in_1   : in  std_logic;
         -- Outputs
         out_1  : out std_logic
       );
end entity dflop_n_reset;

architecture dflop_n_reset_arch of dflop_n_reset is
begin
   Reg_Proc: process (clk, reset)
   begin
      if (reset = '1') then
         out_1 <= '0';
      elsif rising_edge(clk) then
         out_1 <= in_1;
      end if;
   end process;

end architecture dflop_n_reset_arch;
```

D-flop with reset

Pressing on, we now add more functionality to our nascent register. Here we introduce two synchronous controls: an enable, and a low-active synchronous clear. We forgo a timing diagram since the operation is self-evident.

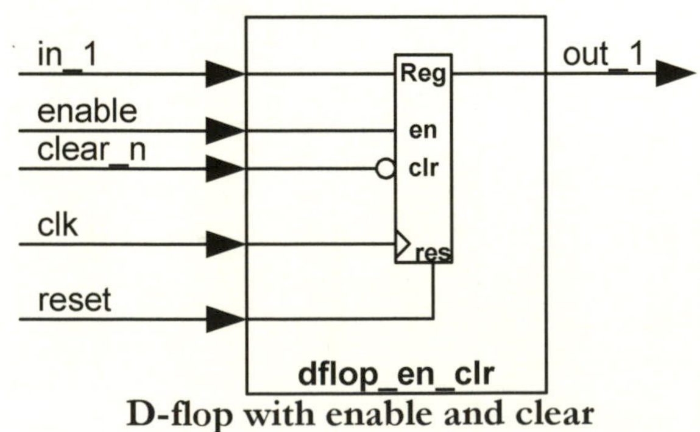

D-flop with enable and clear

Note that the asynchronous reset remains. Besides benefiting from simple consistency, this demonstrates an important point about FPGA design in general: we invariably choose one reset method (synchronous or asynchronous), which is then used globally on all the registers. At a minimum, global resets are necessary for simulation, but additionally may be a practical necessity for proper testing in-circuit. In our case, we will always be using a global asynchronous reset. We should also note that on very large and/or fast designs, the global reset may be segmented into functional domains, but the premise that every flop shares a (semi)common reset remains.

The process statement in the code below expands with the additional synchronous control functions. The asynchronous reset still takes priority (it comes first), but now we've added nested if/else statements. Everything that happens within the "elsif rising_edge(clk)" is synchronous with the clock (clk), since the associated assignments are only executed at rising clock edges. When the input "clear_n" is zero, the output "out_1" is forced to zero (at the next rising edge clock), thus implementing a synchronous clear. Only when the synchronous clear is inactive, and the input "enable" is one is the input "in_1" clocked to the output. Since the synchronous clear comes before the enable, it takes priority; only when the clear is inactive, can the enable allow the input to be clocked to the output.

```
-- -----------------------------------------------
-- Header information
-- -----------------------------------------------
library IEEE;
use IEEE.STD_LOGIC_1164.all;

entity dflop_en_clr is
  port (
         -- Inputs
         clk     : in  std_logic;
         reset   : in  std_logic;
         clear_n : in  std_logic;
         enable  : in  std_logic;
         in_1    : in  std_logic;
         -- Outputs
         out_1   : out std_logic
```

```
      );
end entity dflop_en_clr;

architecture dflop_en_clr_arch of dflop_en_clr is

begin
    --------------- Design implementation --------

   Reg_Proc: process (clk, reset)
   begin
      if (reset = '1') then
         out_1 <= '0';
      elsif rising_edge(clk) then

         if (clear_n = '0') then
            out_1 <= '0';
         elsif (enable = '1') then
            out_1 <= in_1;
         end if;

      end if;
   end process;

end architecture dflop_en_clr_arch;
```

Note what would happen if we reversed the order of the synchronous clear and enable. If that section of the code looked like this:

```
         if (enable = '1') then
            out_1 <= in_1;
         elsif (clear_n = '0') then
            out_1 <= '0';
         end if;
```

then the clear would only be effective when the enable was inactive. That's clearly not what you would expect when looking at the block diagram above.

But what if we wanted the synchronous clear to be gated by the enable input? What if we wanted the enable to enable all synchronous functions? We've already nested the synchronous signals within the "rising_edge(clk)" elsif section, we can continue nesting. Look what happens in the "dflop_sync_enable" code that follows when we subsume the synchronous clear into the enable condition:

```
-- ----------------------------------------------------
-- Header information
-- ----------------------------------------------------
library IEEE;
use IEEE.STD_LOGIC_1164.all;

entity dflop_sync_enable is
  port (
         -- Inputs
         clk     : in  std_logic;
         reset   : in  std_logic;
         clear_n : in  std_logic;
         enable  : in  std_logic;
         in_1    : in  std_logic;
         -- Outputs
         out_1   : out std_logic
       );
end entity dflop_sync_enable;

architecture  dflop_sync_enable_arch  of  dflop_sync_enable
is

begin
    --------------- Design implementation --------

   Reg_Proc: process (clk, reset)
   begin
      if (reset = '1') then
         out_1 <= '0';
      elsif rising_edge(clk) then

         if (enable = '1') then

            if (clear_n = '0') then
               out_1 <= '0';
            else
               out_1 <= in_1;
            end if;

         end if;

      end if;
   end process;

end architecture dflop_sync_enable_arch;
```

Now the synchronous clear is only effective when the enable signal is active. It still takes priority over the registration of "in_1", but the enable now becomes the master activation control over all synchronous operations.

A word about "else". It's a little word, but it can have dire consequences if not given careful attention. In the previous code we note that the final nested registration of the input to the output (out_1 <= in_1;) is located within an "else" condition. This makes sense, since when the dflop is enabled, we want it to do *something*, either clear or register the input. But notice that there is no "else" clause at the top of the if/elsif hierarchy. Here we only want to take action when the asynchronous reset is active or the clock has transitioned high. If we had included an "else" here, our dflop would no longer be a clocked register, but more like a combinatorial operation (in reality, although that code might simulate, the synthesizer tool would likely choke).

We now introduce a few common state-type operations to show how increasingly sophisticated register-based functions are implemented in process statements. A four-bit counter is enabled by a "start" event, and stopped by a "stop" event. The SR flop allows the start and stop events to be short, e.g. one-clock pulses, rather than a continuously enabling flag. Additionally, for further illustration, we delay the start signal two clocks and provide it as an output.

You'll notice that we have not shown the asynchronous reset in the diagram. This is done for clarity; from this point forward it is assumed. It is implemented in the code, and always will be (in this book).

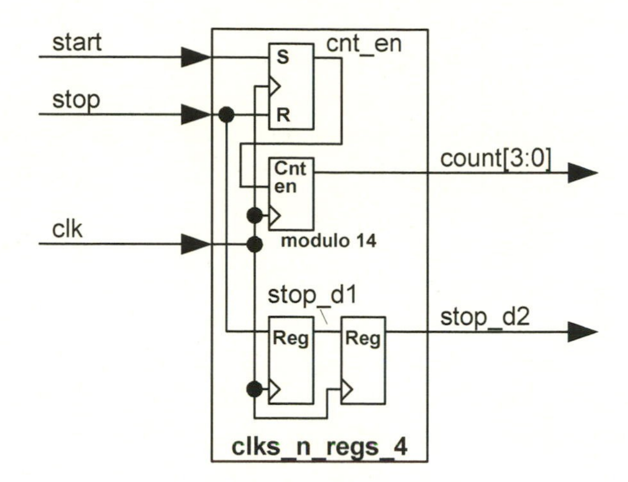

SR flop and counter

The code (clks_n_regs_4) includes two signal declarations for internal signals (cnt_en and stop_d1). We now have multiple register operations within the same process, one for each box in the diagram above: an SR flop, a counter, and the two delays. The SR flop needs no explanation beyond noting that there is no "else" statement, resulting in a latch function (which is indeed what we desire). The counter also has no "else" statement, but since it is an enabled counter, it is also in a sense a latch. Since the counter is modulo 14, the first nested "if" statement clears it when the count is 13, i.e., hex "D". And here we pause to explain that X"..." denotes a hex value. We could have written the "D" as "1101". Note that the same hex format is used to clear the counter in the reset section.

A niggle warning: the X"..." only works for full nibbles. So, there is no problem when the vector size is evenly divisible by four, but if not—say the signal is "std_logic_vector(9 downto 0)" —then we would have to concatenate the regular bit format with the hex format, thus: "00" & X"00". If the value was 0x234, then it would be "10" & X"34". Alternatively, of course, it could be "1000110100".

The actual counting assignment is straightforward, since we just add a one to the current count each clock period that the counter is enabled. There is a complication, however. VHDL in itself does not implement addition. We have to introduce another IEEE library for that—IEEE.NUMERIC_STD. However, it does not do addition to a std_logic_vector signal. Rather, we have to use a new signal type "unsigned" (as you guessed, there is also "signed", but we don't need that for a straight counter). Further, entity IO signals cannot be of the "unsigned" type, but must be of the form std_logic or std_logic_vector. Therefore, we are forced to implement the counter using a local "unsigned" signal, and then convert that to a std_logic_vector type—this is done in the final combinatorial assignment. Note that both signals (here "count" and "count_us") must be of the same width.

I would be disingenuous if I did not mention that there are any number of libraries that have been created over the years and are readily available for download. One such, "STD_Logic_arith" allows arithmetic operations directly on std_logic_vector types, but I have chosen not to use it, since much of the VHDL development world frowns on these non-standardized libraries.

Finally, even if we did not have to re-assign the internal "count_us" unsigned signal to the output std_logic_vector type, we would still have had to use a local signal for the counter, and then re-assign it for the output. This is because VHDL does not allow an output std_logic or std_logic_vector type signal to be re-used locally, and that is exactly what we do when incrementing a counter (e.g., "count_us <= count_us + 1;").

```
-- ------------------------------------------------
-- Header information
-- ------------------------------------------------
library IEEE;
use IEEE.STD_LOGIC_1164.all;
use IEEE.NUMERIC_STD.all;

entity clks_n_regs_4 is
  port ( -- Inputs
         clk       : in  std_logic;
         rst       : in  std_logic;

         start     : in  std_logic;
         stop      : in  std_logic;
         -- Outputs
         count     : out std_logic_vector(3 downto 0);
```

```
            stop_d2    : out std_logic
        );
end entity clks_n_regs_4;

architecture clks_n_regs_4_arch of clks_n_regs_4 is

   signal cnt_en    : std_logic;
   signal count_us  : unsigned(3 downto 0);
   signal stop_d1   : std_logic;

begin
    --------------- Design implementation --------

   Reg_Proc: process (clk, rst)
   begin
      if (rst = '1') then
         cnt_en     <=  '0';
         count_us   <= X"0";
         stop_d1    <=  '0';
         stop_d2    <=  '0';
      elsif rising_edge(clk) then

         -- SR flop
         if (start = '1') then
            cnt_en <= '1';
         elsif (stop = '1') then
            cnt_en <= '0';
         end if;

         -- counter
         if (cnt_en = '1') then
            if (count_us = X"D") then
               count_us <= X"0";
            else
               count_us <= count_us + 1;
            end if;
         end if;

         -- two delays
         stop_d1 <= stop;
         stop_d2 <= stop_d1;

      end if;
   end process;

   count <= std_logic_vector(count_us);

end architecture clks_n_regs_4_arch;
```

SR flop and counter

We'll take this opportunity to introduce an alternative to "signal" declarations. This is the "variable", and it differs from a signal in that a variable is local to just the process where it is used, meaning that it has no reference outside the process, and cannot be used other than inside the process. The following code implements the same operation as the previous clks_n_regs_4.vhd (or almost, as we'll see), except that it replaces the "cnt_en" and "stop_d1" signals with variables of the same name.

```
-- ------------------------------------------------
-- Header information
-- ------------------------------------------------
library IEEE;
use IEEE.STD_LOGIC_1164.all;
use IEEE.NUMERIC_STD.all;


entity clks_n_regs_5 is
  port (
         -- Inputs
         clk       : in  std_logic;
         rst       : in  std_logic;

         start     : in  std_logic;
         stop      : in  std_logic;
         -- Outputs
         count     : out std_logic_vector(3 downto 0);
         stop_d2   : out std_logic
       );
end entity clks_n_regs_5;

architecture clks_n_regs_5_arch of clks_n_regs_5 is

   signal count_us    : unsigned(3 downto 0);

begin
    --------------- Design implementation --------

   Reg_Proc: process (clk, rst)
      variable cnt_en    : std_logic;
      variable stop_d1   : std_logic;
   begin
      if (rst = '1') then
         cnt_en     :=  '0';
         count_us   <= X"0";
         stop_d1    :=  '0';
         stop_d2    <=  '0';
      elsif rising_edge(clk) then
```

```
         -- SR flop
         if (start = '1') then
            cnt_en := '1';
         elsif (stop = '1') then
            cnt_en := '0';
         end if;

         -- counter
         if (cnt_en = '1') then
            if (count_us = X"D") then
               count_us <= X"0";
            else
               count_us <= count_us + 1;
            end if;
         end if;

         -- two delays
         stop_d1 := stop;
         stop_d2 <= stop_d1;

      end if;
   end process;

   count <= std_logic_vector(count_us);

end architecture clks_n_regs_5_arch;
```

SR flop and counter, using variables

We are able to replace these signals with variables, since they are used exclusively within the process. Notice that the variable declarations are made within the process statement rather than the beginning of the architecture. You can see that within this process we use variables in the same way as their predecessor signals of clks_n_regs_4.vhd. There is one very key difference between signals and variables, however: a variable takes on its assignment immediately, while the signal assignment waits until the next rising clock edge. The difference is fundamental, and results in a different behavior in this example. When "count_us" is a signal, here's what the result is after "rst" goes low (assuming "start" is already set):

after 1st clock: count = "0000"
after 2nd clock: count = "0001"

This is because "cnt_en" must be set high with the first clock before the counter is enabled.

But using a variable for "count_us", here's what we get:

after 1st clock: count = "0001"
after 2nd clock: count = "0010"

This happens because as a variable, "cnt_en" is set within the process immediately, and the counter is enabled on the very first clock. If the "cnt_en" assignment were moved after the counter, then the operation would be the same as clks_n_regs_4.vhd.

So why use variables if the operation is so finicky about the placement in the process? The main reason has to do with tool efficiency with very large designs (e.g., variables use less memory than signals in the simulation), and thus has very little to offer you, the small-to-medium size designer, and I suggest that you have the advantage to put them aside for synthesis. Note that since variables are local to processes, the same name could be re-used in different processes. I don't view this as an advantage, but rather the opposite, and another reason you can happily forgo their use.

A final word about sequential versus concurrent operation before moving on. If your background is software, then you are completely used to sequential operation; your code executes one line at a time. Modern processors have dual and quad cores that run concurrently, but we think of them more as multiple computers running side by side, each still executing code that is sequential. FPGAs, of course, are very different, and your VHDL code is translated into gates and registers that all sit there side by side, continuously ready to do their tasks. Combinatorial assignments in your code (outside process statements) do occur concurrently. Operations within a process statement, however, execute sequentially. Generally this fact is not important when we use process statements to create registers (and register-based operations, such as counters). This is because execution occurs at a virtual point in time (the clock edge, assuming we're using signals and not variables), which results in a type of sequential operation that is expected and intended. If I had these two lines of assignment outside a process statement:

```
c <= b;
b <= a;
```

and "a" changed, then both "b" and "c" would also change at the same time. If these same assignments were within a clocked process statement, then "b" would take the value of "a" at one clock edge, and then "c" would follow on the next clock edge. This is exactly what we would expect from two registers: "a"-to-"b", followed by "b"-to-"c".

If these same two assignments were located within a non-clocked process statement, however, the result could be completely different and perhaps unexpected. If instead of a clocked process, we were implementing, for example, a level-enabled latch, then we could end up with "c" holding the original value of "b", while "b" now has transitioned to "a". This is the case whether using signals or variables. However, if we were to just reverse the order of the lines like so:

```
b <= a;
c <= b;
```

now, because of the sequential nature, the level-enabled latch could end up with both "b" and "c" transitioning to "a".

You can avoid unintended operation by containing multiple assignments that are made to the same signal within one conditional sequence. The "contained" conditional sequence could be nested within a larger conditional statement, as long as the final signal assignments are all made together in the same conditional sequence.

The following is an example of how we would NOT want to code:

```
if(a = b and c = '0') then
   out_sig <= in_sig1 AND in_sig2;
end if;

if(a = b and c = '1') then
   out_sig <= in_sig1 OR in_sig2;
end if;
```

This in itself would work okay, but we prefer this:

```
if(a = b and c = '0') then
   out_sig <= in_sig1 AND in_sig2;
elsif(a = b and c = '1') then
   out_sig <= in_sig1 OR in_sig2;
end if;
```

Or, better yet, perhaps this way:

```
if (a=b) then
   if (c = '0') then
      out_sig <= in_sig1 AND in_sig2;
   else
      out_sig <= in_sig1 OR in_sig2;
   end if;
end if;
```

The important point is to ask yourself whether it is possible for any two assignments to potentially be active at the clock edge. If so, restructure the code.

State Machines

Everybody loves state machines, particularly people trying to understand your design. But the clarity is only as effective as how well the coding language communicates the state machine's structure. As we'll see, if coded with proper care to outline the operation, VHDL provides a very good vehicle.

We'll use a fairly simple machine as shown in the diagram below to demonstrate how they can be coded in VHDL. After receiving a "go" event, the state machine transitions from the "idle" state to "active," where it waits while an auxiliary counter steps through a hundred clocks. Once this defined active duration is complete, the state machine returns to "idle," but passes through one last "finish" state on the way. This "finish" state produces a one-clock pulse on the "done" output signal. An external "kill" signal can terminate the wait active duration, forcing the state machine back to idle. For the sake of stability, though, the state machine first waits in an "abort" state until the kill signal goes back inactive.

Note that this design assumes that the inputs are synchronized to the clock that drives the FPGA. Otherwise, the inputs would need to be clocked through an input register (i.e., synchronized) before presentation to the state machine to prevent spurious operation. In fact, if the extra state latency is not an issue, inputs are often re-clocked as standard procedure.

The "done" register is included to avoid combinatorial decode glitches. Gray or one-hot state coding could be used instead, but including an output register provides a more universal application.

You may recognize that the entire operation of this sample design could be implemented with just the counter alone (enabling and clearing it directly with the external signals), but the state machine presents a clear communication of the intent of the circuit, and also provides an easy avenue for later changes or expansion.

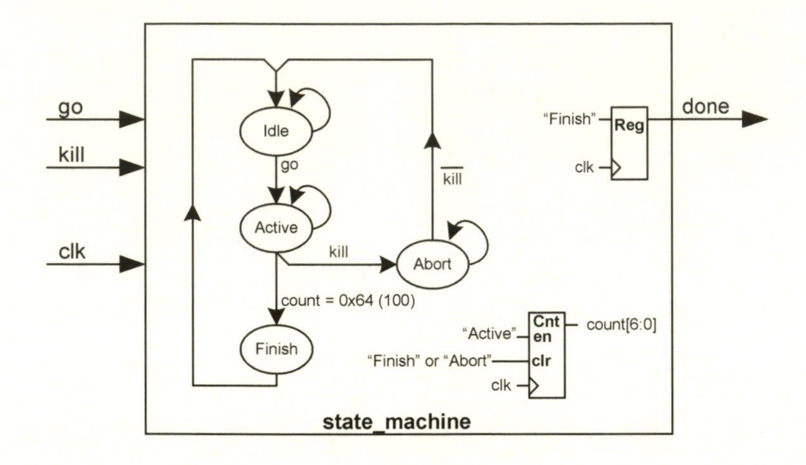

State Machine

```
-- ------------------------------------------------------
-- Header information
-- ------------------------------------------------------
library IEEE;
use IEEE.STD_LOGIC_1164.all;
use IEEE.NUMERIC_STD.all;

entity state_machine is
  port (
         -- Inputs
         clk        : in  std_logic;
         reset      : in  std_logic;

         go         : in  std_logic;
         kill       : in  std_logic;
         -- Outputs
         done       : out std_logic
       );
end entity state_machine;

architecture state_machine_arch of state_machine is

   signal count     : unsigned(7 downto 0);

   type state_labels is  (  Idle,
                            Active,
                            Finish,
                            Abort
                         );
```

```
   signal state_reg  : state_labels;

begin
    --------------- Design implementation --------

   State_Proc: process (clk, reset)
   begin
     if (reset = '1') then
        state_reg  <=  Idle;
     elsif rising_edge(clk) then

       case (state_reg) is

         when Idle =>

           if (go = '1') then          state_reg <= Active;
           end if;

         when Active =>

           if (kill = '1') then        state_reg <= Abort;
           elsif (count = X"64") then state_reg <= Finish;
           end if;

         when Finish =>                state_reg <= Idle;

         when Abort =>

           if (kill /= '1') then       state_reg <= Idle;
           end if;

         when others =>                state_reg <= Idle;

       end case;

     end if;
   end process;

   Reg_Proc: process (clk, reset)
   begin
      if (reset = '1') then
         count  <= X"00";
         done   <=   '0';
      elsif rising_edge(clk) then

         -- duration counter
         if (   state_reg = Finish
             OR state_reg = Abort
            ) then
            count <= X"00";
         elsif (state_reg = Active) then
            count <= count + 1;
```

```
         end if;

         -- output register
         if (state_reg = Finish) then
            done <= '1';
         else
            done <= '0';
         end if;

      end if;
   end process;

end architecture state_machine_arch;
```

State Machine

State machines have limited effectiveness if we are not able to use human-friendly labels, and VHDL provides a handy method. I previously explained that the STD_LOGIC_1164 library defines the std_logic type signals, and I also explained that designers can write and include their own libraries. Well, VHDL allows you (the designer) to also define signal types in the body of the architecture (among other places). We will use this feature to label the state machine. This is done in the line that starts with "type", which is the keyword for defining our own types. This is followed by "state_labels", which is the name I've decided on for this new type (it could have been "goose"). The "is" is a keyword, followed by the list of component values of my new type (that I've made up), separated by commas and enclosed in parenthesis. There are a variety of types in VHDL, and this one is called an enumerated type, which in our case consists of a list of abstract labels. Our application of our new type is narrowly limited to defining the state machine states—custom labels for a specific use.

I should explain that although we will be using these abstract labels in the coding, the synthesizer tool will convert them into registered logic signals—either vector values (e.g., Idle = "00", Active = "01", etc.) or a one-hot structure, where each state is represented by a different register. But this is invisible to us at the coding and simulation level.

The type declaration is followed by the actual state machine signal declaration. Instead of std_logic, our state machine signal is of type state_labels that we ourselves have defined.

Although the implementation of the state machine could be included in the same process statement as the rest of the registered logic, I like to keep it separated ("State_proc", here); a recognition that its workings are fundamental to understanding the overall operation. The state machine itself is implemented using a case statement. Case statements are familiar if you have experience with almost any type of programming, but in a nutshell, the case statement selects and executes the statement group (identified after keyword "when" and before the required "=>") that matches the value inside the parenthesis ("state_reg" in this example). Since the case statement is contained inside a clocked process, an assessment and one selected group is executed each clock.

We'll follow through some of the operation for demonstration. We start with the state machine in the idle state, where "state_reg" contains the "Idle" label. Each clock, the case selection executes Idle, where if "go" is not high (not active) then nothing is done, so that for the next clock "state_reg" still contains "Idle." Eventually "go" transitions high, and "state_reg" is assigned "Active". This corresponds to the first transition of the state machine. For the next clock, the case statement selects for execution the Active state, where "state_reg" remains unchanged until either "kill" goes high, or the counter reaches its terminal value (0x64, or decimal 100), when the state machine then transitions to Abort or Finish respectively. Note that the "if then" structures within the conditional states (the ones that don't just immediately jump away like Finish to Idle) include no "else" component. If there were an "else", it would instruct the machine to stay at this state. Leaving it out implies the same thing.

We'll not detail the entire machine operation, as you've surely gotten the gist by now. Note that instead of leaving the Abort state with "`kill = '0'`", I've indicated the condition as "`kill /= '1'`". Both are equally valid, but the latter coordinates with the nomenclature used in the state machine diagram. We strive to use VHDL both as a tool for defining a design, and as a means to best convey the operation.

And, taking that as a segue, we'll now review the coding structure. Normally we find the assignment statement (e.g. "state_reg <= Active") following the conditional statement on the next line. Here, though, we have it following on the same line. VHDL doesn't care, and this allows for a visually coherent form—the state machine operation is easily understood based on the transition decisions. We note that this is only possible because this process statement contains nothing but the state machine. If it didn't (as we'll soon see), then we would have to squeeze in multiple assignments, ruining the regular matrix structure.

Finally, be aware that, as in the with/select above, many synthesis programs require the "others" statement in the case list, even if the case statement already includes all possible selection branch combinations (considered "full").

The counter and output register of this module are similar to those we've already seen. Note that we decode state machine states directly in these blocks using the "state_reg" register signal and associated labels. Also note that I've set the clear conditions of the counter to match the diagram above (via the "Finish" and "Abort" states), but the following works equally well, and in fact, has the advantage of defining the state of the counter completely to include the "Idle" state (by default):

```
-- duration counter
if (state_reg = Active) then
   count <= count + 1;
else
   count <= X"00";
end if;
```

Finally, note that although the counter is seven bits, I've declared it as eight. This is a convenience so that I can use the shortened X"00" form of expression instead of "00000000". Since the eighth bit (the MSb) is not actually used, the synthesis tool will strip it away anyway.

As we've noted, VHDL code can be structured in a variety of ways. Some designers might prefer the auxiliary counter and output register to be collected into one process statement along with the state machine. This is how it might look:

```
-- -----------------------------------------------------
-- Header information
-- -----------------------------------------------------
library IEEE;
use IEEE.STD_LOGIC_1164.all;
use IEEE.NUMERIC_STD.all;

entity state_machine_2 is
  port ( -- Inputs
         clk        : in  std_logic;
         reset      : in  std_logic;

         go         : in  std_logic;
         kill       : in  std_logic;
         -- Outputs
         done       : out std_logic
       );
end entity state_machine_2;

architecture state_machine_2_arch of state_machine_2 is

   signal count     : unsigned(7 downto 0);

   type state_labels is  (  Idle,
                            Active,
                            Finish,
                            Abort
                         );

   signal state_reg  : state_labels;

begin
    --------------- Design implementation --------
   Combined_Proc: process (clk, reset)
   begin
      if (reset = '1') then
         state_reg  <=  Idle;
         count      <= X"00";
         done       <=   '0';
      elsif rising_edge(clk) then

         case (state_reg) is

            when Idle =>

               if (go = '1') then
                  state_reg <= Active;
               end if;

               count <= X"00";
               done  <=   '0';
```

```
            when Active =>

               count <= count + 1;
               done  <= '0';

               if (kill = '1') then
                  state_reg <= Abort;
               elsif (count = X"64") then
                  state_reg <= Finish;
               end if;

            when Finish =>

               count <= X"00";
               done  <=   '1';

               state_reg <= Idle;

            when Abort =>

               count <= X"00";
               done  <=   '0';

               if (kill /= '1') then
                  state_reg <= Idle;
               end if;

            when others =>

               count <= X"00";
               done  <=   '0';
               state_reg <= Idle;

         end case;
      end if;
   end process;
end architecture state_machine_2_arch;
```

State Machine, combined process statement

Besides losing the visual advantage of easily correlating the state machine decisions with corresponding actions, this type of code structure is susceptible to mis-operation if care isn't taken to account for every register state in every case selection. Although often resulting in code that is not as tight, when each function is implemented with its own process, each operation is clear and concise.

Modular Design

The design examples we've used so far have been very small for obvious reasons. Designs of increasing complexity reach a point where containing them in a single file becomes cumbersome. At some point sheer size compels us to break up the design into component parts, possibly multiple layers of hierarchy.

There are other good reasons besides just size, though, to use a modular approach:

o reuse (components of a design can be used in multiple places without repeating all the code details);

o pre-existing designs (code developed elsewhere can be incorporated as a "black box" without caring about constituent details);

o clarity (the code can be segmented into functional pieces that correspond to blocks described in high level descriptions);

o simulation (individual pieces of the design can often times be simulated more rigorously and completely than when embedded in the larger operation);

o changes (by compartmentalizing the functioning, the consequences of changes can be studied and simulated in isolation).

Now having effused about the benefits of modular design, I immediately offer caution against overuse. Keep in mind that anyone examining your code will need to navigate through as many files as there are modules. No one will love you if you break out every register, mux, and counter as its own instantiated module, when the associated process statement would have taken no more room than the instantiated module that's replacing it.

With that admonishment out of the way, we can proceed to look at how modules are instantiated within other modules—in the case of VHDL, "components" within architectures.

For the first example, we will use the design from the previous section (State Machines) for our internal instantiated module (i.e., component). Note that there were two coded versions of that, but since they operate exactly the same, and have the same input/outputs, we could use either one.

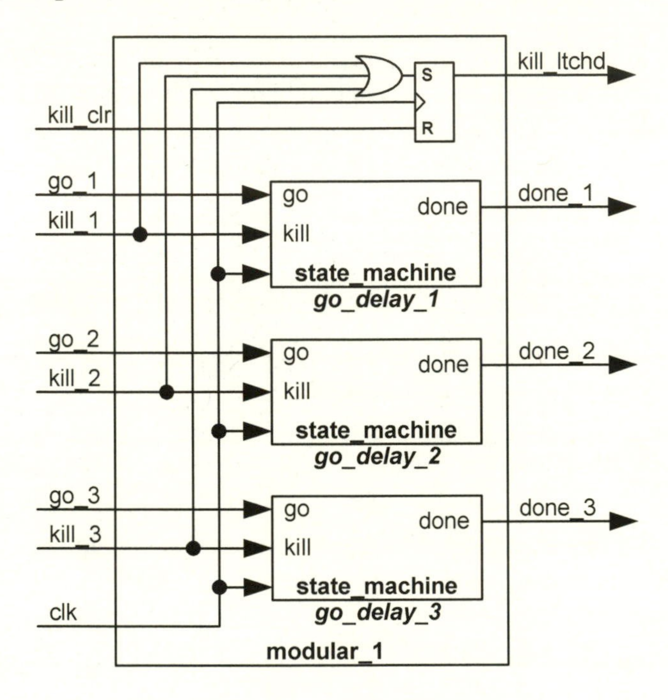

First Modular Example

Here, we've instantiated three copies of the state_machine component in a new higher-level module (sometimes called a "wrapper" when most of the code consists of instantiated sub-modules) called "modular_1". We've labeled the first instantiated copy as "go_delay_1", the second as "go_delay_2", and the third as "go_delay_3". Additionally, we've also added an SR latch to detect if any of the modules' internal counts were "killed," and have provided a signal (kill_clr) to clear the latch.

On the next page is the code file for "modular_1".

```
-- ---------------------------------------------------
-- Header information
-- ---------------------------------------------------
library IEEE;
use IEEE.STD_LOGIC_1164.all;
use IEEE.NUMERIC_STD.all;

entity modular_1 is
  port (
        -- Inputs
        clk          : in  std_logic;
        reset        : in  std_logic;

        kill_clr     : in  std_logic;

        go_1         : in  std_logic;
        kill_1       : in  std_logic;
        go_2         : in  std_logic;
        kill_2       : in  std_logic;
        go_3         : in  std_logic;
        kill_3       : in  std_logic;

        -- Outputs
        kill_ltchd   : out std_logic;
        done_1       : out std_logic;
        done_2       : out std_logic;
        done_3       : out std_logic
      );
end entity modular_1;

architecture modular_1_arch of modular_1 is

   component state_machine
     port (
           -- Inputs
           clk          : in  std_logic;
           reset        : in  std_logic;

           go           : in  std_logic;
           kill         : in  std_logic;
           -- Outputs
           done         : out std_logic
         );
   end component;

begin
    --------------- Design implementation --------

  Go_Delay_1: state_machine
  port map
      (
```

```
         -- Inputs
         clk          => clk,
         reset        => reset,

         go           => go_1,
         kill         => kill_1,
         -- Outputs
         done         => done_1
      );

   Go_Delay_2: state_machine
   port map
      (
         -- Inputs
         clk          => clk,
         reset        => reset,

         go           => go_2,
         kill         => kill_2,
         -- Outputs
         done         => done_2
      );

   Go_Delay_3: state_machine
   port map
      (
         -- Inputs
         clk          => clk,
         reset        => reset,

         go           => go_3,
         kill         => kill_3,
         -- Outputs
         done         => done_3
      );


    Reg_Proc: process (clk, reset)
    begin
       if (reset = '1') then
          kill_ltchd   <=   '0';
       elsif rising_edge(clk) then

          if (   kill_1 = '1'
              OR kill_2 = '1'
              OR kill_3 = '1'
             ) then
             kill_ltchd <= '1';
          elsif (kill_clr = '1') then
             kill_ltchd <= '0';
          end if;
```

```
        end if;
    end process;

end architecture modular_1_arch;
```

First Modular Example

First, like the signals we've already seen, we must declare the components that we will be instantiating before "begin". In this case, that is just the one state machine module. Notice that the component declaration is very similar to the entity declaration of "state_machine"—essentially a list of I/O signals. In fact, an easy way to create the component declaration is to first copy the entity declaration from the file of the component you are instantiating. Then:

1) replace "entity" with "component";

2) delete "is";

3) for the last line, replace "end entity [name of entity]" with "end component".

The entire architecture design consists of three lower-level component instantiations, followed by one process statement for the SR latch.

Each component instantiation includes:

o a label for this component instantiation (e.g., "Go_Delay_1"), followed by a colon, followed by the name of the component (that we declared above);

o the key words "port map";

o the port map—an I/O connection list—enclosed in parenthesis, where the connections are made between the instantiat-<u>ing</u> architecture and the instantiat-<u>ed</u> component;

o a semi-colon to end the instantiation.

In the port map, the names on the left side of the "=>" connection symbol correspond to the name of the port signal of the instantiat-<u>ed</u> component—this must match the names in the declaration above. The names on the right side of the "=>" connection symbol correspond to the local signal names of the instantiat-ing architecture. Note that each connection signal pair is separated by a comma (but not after the last one).

In this first example, we note that, since all the signals connect directly between the "modular_1" entity input and output ports and the instantiated components, we do not have any local signals to declare.

Next, we make a minor change to our example modular design. Each module stage now ORs its "go" input with the previous stage's "done" output.

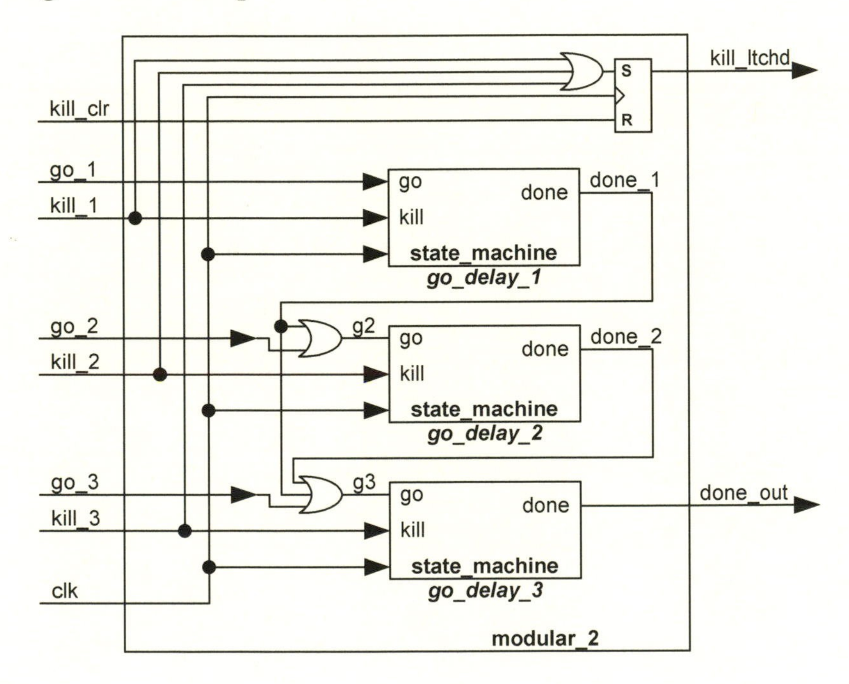

Second Modular Example

```
-- ------------------------------------------------
-- Header information
-- ------------------------------------------------
library IEEE;
use IEEE.STD_LOGIC_1164.all;
use IEEE.NUMERIC_STD.all;

entity modular_2 is
  port (
       -- Inputs
       clk          : in  std_logic;
       reset        : in  std_logic;

       kill_clr     : in  std_logic;

       go_1         : in  std_logic;
       kill_1       : in  std_logic;
       go_2         : in  std_logic;
       kill_2       : in  std_logic;
       go_3         : in  std_logic;
       kill_3       : in  std_logic;

       -- Outputs
       kill_ltchd   : out std_logic;
       done_3       : out std_logic
      );
end entity modular_2;

architecture modular_2_arch of modular_2 is

   component state_machine
     port (
          -- Inputs
          clk        : in  std_logic;
          reset      : in  std_logic;

          go         : in  std_logic;
          kill       : in  std_logic;
          -- Outputs
          done       : out std_logic
         );
   end component;

   signal done_1    : std_logic;
   signal g2        : std_logic;
   signal done_2    : std_logic;
   signal g3        : std_logic;

begin
    --------------- Design implementation --------
```

```
Go_Delay_1: state_machine
port map
    (
       -- Inputs
       clk        => clk,
       reset      => reset,

       go         => go_1,
       kill       => kill_1,
       -- Outputs
       done       => done_1
    );

g2 <= (done_1 OR go_2);

Go_Delay_2: state_machine
port map
    (
       -- Inputs
       clk        => clk,
       reset      => reset,

       go         => g2,
       kill       => kill_2,
       -- Outputs
       done       => done_2
    );

g3 <= (done_1 OR done_2 OR go_3);

Go_Delay_3: state_machine
port map
    (
       -- Inputs
       clk        => clk,
       reset      => reset,

       go         => g3,
       kill       => kill_3,
       -- Outputs
       done       => done_3
    );


 Reg_Proc: process (clk, reset)
 begin
    if (reset = '1') then
       kill_ltchd <= '0';
    elsif rising_edge(clk) then

       if (   kill_1 = '1'
           OR kill_2 = '1'
```

```
            OR kill_3 = '1'
           ) then
           kill_ltchd <= '1';
        elsif (kill_clr = '1') then
           kill_ltchd <= '0';
        end if;

     end if;
  end process;

end architecture modular_2_arch;
```

Second Modular Example

Notice that the "done_1" and "done_2" outputs of the first example design now become local signals, and are declared as such. Additionally, we declare intermediate logic signals "g1" and "g2".

A side note: a newer version of VHDL (VHDL-2008) allows logic operations as part of the port map, like so:

```
Go_Delay_2: state_machine
port map
    (
       -- Inputs
       clk        => clk,
       reset      => reset,

       go         => (done_1 OR go_2),
       kill       => kill_2,
       -- Outputs
       done       => done_2
    );
```

Here, the intermediate "g2" signal is eliminated. Not all simulation and/or synthesis tools support this version yet, so you may still be stuck with the more verbose method.

Instantiated modules are not limited to your own VHDL code, or even to code that was written by another designer of your acquaintance. Instantiating sub-modules is the method we use to incorporate a variety of functionality delivered as tested and documented components. These include "IP cores"—code, sometimes quite substantial and complex, provided (often sold) by third-parties that implement a well-defined set of functions. Common examples of cores are complete micro-processors. You could, if you wanted, include a PowerPC™ in your design. Other examples of off-the-shelf cores are PCIe interfaces, video encoder/decoders, encryption blocks for data security (e.g., DES and AES), and error detection/correction (e.g., Viterbi and Reed-Solomon). There are probably as many IP cores as there are useful segmentable functions. Many are available from the FPGA vendor directly. Some are fixed, straight-forward functional blocks, such as 8b/10b encoder/decoders. Others are synthesized based on designer-provided parameters during the design process by vendor-specific software that comes integrated as part of the FPGA vendor's tool suite, or purchased separately. Examples of these sorts of cores are FFT and FIR filter DSP blocks, Gigabit Ethernet interfaces, and FIFOs.

Another important class of vendor-provided modules is primitive cores. These are functionally simpler blocks that are either built directly into the FPGA device fabric, or are synthesized in a way that utilizes fabric specifics that would not otherwise be visible to general third-party synthesis tools (thus the label primitive). The key difference between primitive cores and the afore-described off-the-shelf IP cores is that, whereas the latter generally consist of VHDL code that becomes a part of the overall synthesized design, primitive cores are just place-markers in the code that the vendor compiler (versus the synthesis stage) recognizes and inserts the proper functionality at the device-specific stage of the path towards a final binary build file. These place-markers are called "black boxes," and have the appearance in the code of a normal instantiated component. However, no associated VHDL file exists to go along with them. In fact, most synthesis software upon encountering an instantiated module for which it cannot find an associated VHDL file will automatically declare it as a black box entity. Designers, as a result, must sometimes routinely scan synthesis results looking for instances of black box declarations in case they are simply the result of lost or misplaced VHDL files.

Primitive cores will be addressed again in the next section on memories.

Memories

Memories are an important component in many fields of digital design, and they come in a variety of forms: DRAM, SDRAM, DDR, QDR, SRAM, FIFO, LIFO, DP, etc.. Of these, the first four are of course not (yet) available for FPGA implementation, but almost any other form imaginable has probably been implemented. Memory design in FPGAs is another topic that could be a whole book unto itself, and here we will simply review the fundamentals of designing memories using VHDL.

Memories implemented inside FPGAs (versus memory controllers, which would also include the DRAMs, etc.) can be defined in three general ways:

1) infer the memory directly via the VHDL code;

2) build the memory using the vendor's primitive RAM structures;

3) design the memory using the FPGA vendor's specialized tools.

We'll discuss the last two first. The second option (primitive RAM structures) uses RAM resources that are built into the FPGA device fabric, and thus are the most efficient means of building memory functions (and if you don't use them, then they represent valuable substrate that goes unused). Each RAM block occupies a fixed amount of FPGA die, and they usually have a limited degree of flexibility as to their depth versus width (aspect ratio). These RAM blocks are an example of primitive cores discussed in the previous section, and as explained there, when using these in a VHDL design, they are instantiated as black box modules. In this mode, it's up to you the designer to build up in VHDL any associated control logic, such as circular addressing for FIFOs, logic for the FIFO depth flags, etc.. Most built-in FPGA RAM blocks can be configured to operate as dual-port memories, vastly simplifying many designs.

The third option (vendor's specialized tools) is by far the easiest approach, particularly with application-specific FIFOs. This method was also discussed in the previous section, and functional blocks built around memories (FIFOs, ROMs, CAMs, etc.) are just an example of the IP cores built using vendor-specific software. The designer, via the GUIs of the vendor software, establishes the parameters of the memory functional block. Parameters for FIFOs, for example, might include depth, input width, output width, various flag locations, etc..

The main downside to using vendor-supplied IP core generators is that they depend on vendor-supplied software. This limits the design's portability, meaning that, should the design be moved to another vendor's device (e.g., migrate to an ASIC), all those IP cores will need to be re-designed, either using the new vendor's IP generation tool, or built up anew in VHDL. Either way, this often translates to a major design and test effort. If, on the other hand, you are confident you will never change FPGA vendors, then this is not an issue.

However, even if you never change FPGA vendors, there still may be issues related to the vendor's IP generation tool evolution. If you knew that you were going to create the design just once and never revisit it again, there would be no problem. But in practice, this almost never happens. Whether from requirement changes introduced later, or subtle problems found down the road that require modifications, inevitably the design sees changes. If the changes manifest in one of the vendor-generated cores, then the IP module will need to be re-generated, and this in turn may require you to use a newer version of the vendor core generation tool. Although rare, there sometimes are differences in how the new tool creates the functions, particularly when the vendor replaces a whole category subset of the tool with a completely "new and improved" version. Also, again though rare, a vendor may completely eliminate support for an esoteric, infrequently used type of core.

Lastly, we go back to the first method of defining memories: inferring the memory directly via the VHDL code. This is the method used when the design is expected, or even suspected, to migrate later to an ASIC, where RAM blocks and convenient GUI-based vendor IP generators are but a rumor. Also, inferred memories are often used for very small memories—specifically, memories significantly smaller than the smallest primitive RAM block (we may be saving those for places where they are really needed).

First, we should explain why we say that the memory is "inferred," and not just implemented in the code like a register or mux. Synthesis tools—whether FPGA or ASIC—include specialized capabilities to recognize when a memory is being implied (AKA inferred). The reason is that the tool can then take advantage of those memory resources at its disposal (specific to the chosen device). In the case of FPGAs, this may ensure that the synthesis tool uses RAM blocks if appropriate (and allowed by the user). Even if primitive IP blocks are not used, the synthesis tool may take special precautions (e.g., coordinated timing) when constructing a memory from VHDL code, but only if it recognizes it as such.

We'll start with a simple dual-port memory. Data flows in one direction, entering from the left through a write port, and accessed from the right via a separate read port.

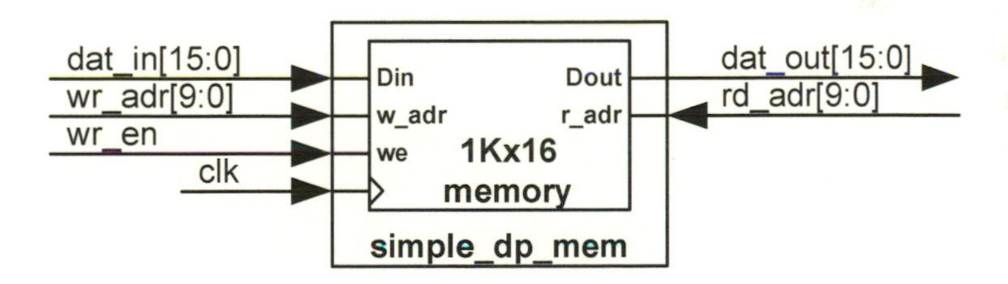

Simple Dual-port Memory

We will implement this as a fully synchronous memory, meaning that both the input and output data are clocked (versus, for example, that the output data changes as soon as the read address changes). This does not mean, however, that the write or read addresses are registered (otherwise, the write address would have to come one clock before the associated data to be written). Therefore, write data (dat_in) is presented to the memory during the same clock as the write address (wr_adr), but the read data (dat_out) appears out of the memory one clock after the read address (rd_adr).

Before we look at the sample code, though, I must first explain that although each synthesis tool may have its own particular requirements associated with inferred memories, one aspect that virtually all have in common is that they expect the memory to be implemented as an array. VHDL supports arrays, but we must define the array before using it. This is a two-step process, and uses the VHDL "type" declaration. First we create an array "type" of the size and width we want, and then we declare that the signal that represents the memory is to be of this type. You may recognize that this is similar to the two-step creation of enumerated states in the previous chapter.

Now for the code:

```
-- -----------------------------------------------
-- Header information
-- -----------------------------------------------
library IEEE;
use IEEE.STD_LOGIC_1164.all;
use IEEE.NUMERIC_STD.all;

entity simple_dp_mem is
  port (
        rst           : in  std_logic;
        clk           : in  std_logic;

        dat_in        : in  std_logic_vector(15 downto 0);
        wr_adr        : in  std_logic_vector(9 downto 0);
        wr_en         : in  std_logic;

        dat_out       : out std_logic_vector(15 downto 0);
        rd_adr        : in  std_logic_vector(9 downto 0)
      );
end entity simple_dp_mem;

architecture simple_dp_mem_arch of simple_dp_mem is

    -- 2D array type for the RAM
    type array_1kx16 is array(1023 downto 0) of
                         std_logic_vector(15 downto 0);

    -- declare the RAM.
    signal ram : array_1kx16;

begin
```

```
    process(clk)
    begin
      if rising_edge(clk) then

        if(wr_en = '1') then
           ram(to_integer(unsigned(wr_adr))) <= dat_in;
           -- Read-during-write returns NEW data
           dat_out <= ram(to_integer(unsigned(rd_adr)));
        else
           -- Read only
           dat_out <= ram(to_integer(unsigned(rd_adr)));
        end if;

      end if;
    end process;

end architecture simple_dp_mem_arch;
```

Simple Dual-port Memory

In the first step in defining the memory, the type name "array_1kx16" is my own, and it could have been "donkey". The "array" is a keyword, and "(1023 downto 0)" defines the array as having 1k (i.e. 1024) elements. Each element of the array is a 16-bit word (of type std_logic_vector). As you've guessed, each array element represents one memory location. A word about the array indexing: you see that I've used [1023:0]—I could have used [1024:1], but a zero-based index is pretty much the standard for memories. Note that I can use a three-bit address word to access a [7:0] memory (000 to 111), but would need four bits to access [8:1] (0001 to 1000).

The second declaration line simply assigns our memory name "ram" (it could have been "lizard") to be our array type.

Looking at the architecture body, we can easily see how the simple synchronous DP memory is implemented. The addresses, both write and read, each point to one location (or word) in the array. If the write enable signal (wr_en) is active, at the rising edge of the clock the write data word (dat_in) is loaded into the array at the location specified by the write address (wr_adr). Simultaneously, the value located at the location specified by the read address (rd_adr) is loaded into the memory's output register (dat_out).

It could have been even simpler had we allowed ourselves to use other, non-standardized libraries, but as it is, we have a rather cumbersome method of using the std_logic_vector input addresses (write and read) as the array index. The index of arrays must be an integer, and the IEEE standard NUMERIC_STD library provides a conversion we can use. Unfortunately, it doesn't convert directly from std_logic_vector to integer. Instead, it converts unsigned values, so we must first convert the std_logic_vector address to an unsigned value, thus the nested parenthesis and conversions. If you've ever heard people say that verilog is easier to learn than VHDL, you may now understand why.

Left to the fate of chance by ambiguity, this code would probably result in the synthesis software using the RAM block resources of the FPGA if available. Explicit direction can be included to direct the synthesis tool to either specifically use RAM blocks or specifically not use RAM blocks (in which case the memory is then referred to as distributed RAM). Each synthesis tool has its own format for these types of embedded directions, and the designer must consult the tool's documentation for guidance. Sometimes the tool uses a configuration option, but often the synthesis directions can be communicated via comments in the VHDL code that include one or more keywords that the tool recognizes (strictly speaking this violates the premise of a comment). Here is an example—this directs the Xilinx XST synthesis software to implement the memory not as RAM blocks, but as distributed RAM:

```
//synthesis attribute ram_style of ram is distributed
```

This comment would be placed just prior to the memory register array declaration. Note that "ram" in the comment is the label of the array in our code.

Note that although "rst" is brought into the module, it is not used in our memory implementation (in fact, it's not used at all, which is permissible in VHDL). This is because RAM blocks, per se, do not have resets. If we wanted to implement the memory as distributed RAM, we would have to consult the vendor's FPGA documentation to see if resets are allowed.

Finally, we need to address a troublesome point regarding the memory's operation when a write and read are made to the same address simultaneously. There are two possibilities: 1) the data that is read is the original value before the write replaced it (called "read-before-write"), or 2) the data is the new value that is being written (called "write-before-read"). Our code implies a write-before-read operation based on the simple fact that the write assignment comes before the read assignment in the process statement (reversing the order would imply a read-before-write). Newer RAM blocks typically accommodate either type of operation, but some older versions are fixed, and in that case, as the designer you would have to make sure your code matches (and that your design operates correctly).

Next, we look at a full dual-port memory, where both ports have both write and read capability.

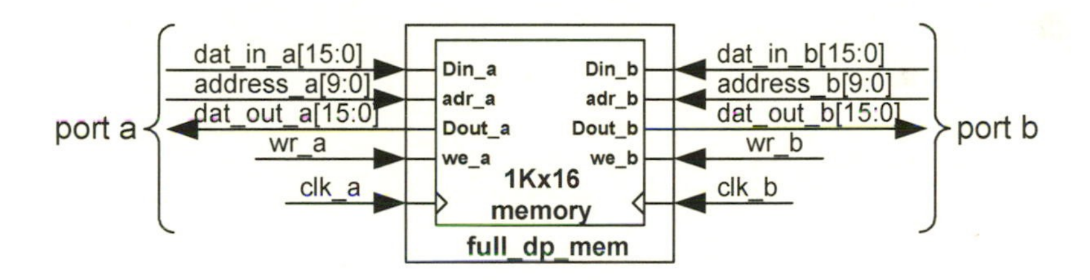

Full Dual-port Memory

As with the simple dual-port memory, this memory is fully synchronous, where write data (dat_in_[a/b]) is presented to the memory during the same clock as the address (address_[a/b]) for writes (when wr_[a/b] is active), but the read data (dat_out_[a/b]) appears out of the memory one clock after the address for reads. If you're not familiar with full dual-port memories, note that data written from either port can be read from either port—the contents of the memory are shared between the two ports. Note that we've also added a second clock, so that each port is now clocked independently (both ports could share a clock if independent clocking is not needed).

```
-- ------------------------------------------------
-- Header information
-- ------------------------------------------------
library IEEE;
use IEEE.STD_LOGIC_1164.all;
use IEEE.NUMERIC_STD.all;

entity full_dp_mem is
  port (
        -- port A
        clk_a         : in  std_logic;
        wr_a          : in  std_logic;
        address_a     : in  std_logic_vector(9 downto 0);
        dat_in_a      : in  std_logic_vector(15 downto 0);
        dat_out_a     : out std_logic_vector(15 downto 0);

        -- port B
        clk_b         : in  std_logic;
        wr_b          : in  std_logic;
        address_b     : in  std_logic_vector(9 downto 0);
        dat_in_b      : in  std_logic_vector(15 downto 0);
        dat_out_b     : out std_logic_vector(15 downto 0)
      );
end entity full_dp_mem;

architecture full_dp_mem_arch of full_dp_mem is

    -- 2D array type for the RAM
    type array_1kx16 is array(1023 downto 0) of
                             std_logic_vector(15 downto 0);

    -- declare the RAM.
    signal ram : array_1kx16;

begin

  process(clk_a)
  begin
    if rising_edge(clk_a) then -- Port A
      if(wr_a = '1') then
         ram(to_integer(unsigned(address_a))) <= dat_in_a;
         -- Read-during-write returns NEW data
         dat_out_a <= dat_in_a;
      else
         -- Read only
         dat_out_a <= ram(to_integer(unsigned(address_a)));
      end if;
    end if;
  end process;

  process(clk_b)
  begin
    if rising_edge(clk_b)  then -- Port B
      if(wr_b = '1') then
         ram(to_integer(unsigned(address_b))) <= dat_in_b;
         -- Read-during-write returns NEW data
         dat_out_b <= dat_in_b;
      else
         -- Read only
```

```
      dat_out_b <= ram(to_integer(unsigned(address_b)));
    end if;
  end if;
end process;

end architecture full_dp_mem_arch;
```

Full Dual-port Memory

For as much complexity as a full-featured dual-port memory contains, the VHDL code is relatively simple. Since each port operates from its own dedicated clock, we use separate identical (other than signal names) process statement for each. Whereas for the simple DP memory, each port was dedicated as either a write or a read, now each port includes both modes. Since each port shares an address for reading and writing, the question arises as to what happens to the read output during write cycles. In the case of this code, the operation is essentially write-before-read, meaning that when wr_[a/b] is active, the data presented on dat_in_[a/b] is copied to the read signal dat_out_[a/b]. However, whereas for the simple DP memory code the write-before-read was implied, here the operation is explicitly defined with the "dat_out_[a/b] <= dat_in_[a/b]" assignment inside the write "if" statement.

Comparing the two process statements, notice that we make assignments to the same signal from within two different process statements—assigning the memory "ram" with write data. This is normally a no-no, and would be as a minimum flagged as a warning by the synthesis software, and possibly as an error. In this case, though, it is appropriate since we are expecting the synthesis software to recognize that the two process statements go together to form one structure (the DP memory).

The dual process statements bring us to a last subject regarding this full dual-port memory: simultaneous accesses to the same address from the two ports (as implemented in the two process statements). This could be two simultaneous writes, or a write and a read. With the previous simple dual-port structure with one clock, we had the means to define what should happen—either write-before-read, or read-before-write. Here, though, because each port operates off its own clock, we have no mechanism in VHDL to describe what should happen. In this case it is up to the synthesis software, and possibly the hardware fabric itself.

Lastly we look at a simple single-port memory—a type that is almost never used in FPGAs in any substantial way. The reason is that FPGA memory, whether RAM blocks or distributed, is based on d-flop registers rather than bona fide memory cell elements. Thus, RAM blocks inherently provide separate write and read ports; in fact, extra logic must be used to implement a single-port memory over a simple dual-port. I present this structure for illustration only.

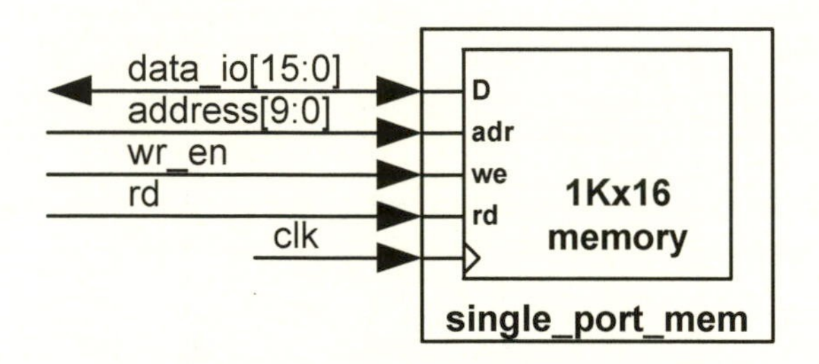

Single-port Memory

Data to be written is presented along with the write address and an active "wr_en" all during the same clock, while for reads, the read address along with an active "rd" are presented during one clock, and the data appears one clock later. Since there is only one port, the data bus is bi-directional (input for writes, output for reads).

```
-- ------------------------------------------------
-- Header information
-- ------------------------------------------------

library IEEE;
use IEEE.STD_LOGIC_1164.all;
use IEEE.NUMERIC_STD.all;

entity single_port_mem is
  port (
        clk      : in    std_logic;

        data_io  : inout std_logic_vector(15 downto 0);
        address  : in    std_logic_vector(9 downto 0);
        wr_en    : in    std_logic;
        rd       : in    std_logic
      );
end entity single_port_mem;

architecture single_port_mem_arch of single_port_mem is

   -- 2D array type for the RAM
   type array_1kx16 is array(1023 downto 0) of
                             std_logic_vector(15 downto 0);

   -- declare the RAM.
   signal ram : array_1kx16;

   -- intermediate RAM output
   signal dat_out     : std_logic_vector(15 downto 0);
   signal rd_d1       : std_logic;

begin

   process(clk)
   begin
     if rising_edge(clk) then

       -- writes

       if(wr_en = '1') then
         ram(to_integer(unsigned(address))) <= data_io;
       end if;

       -- reads

       dat_out <= ram(to_integer(unsigned(address)));

       rd_d1 <= rd;

     end if;
```

```
   end process;

   data_io <= dat_out  when rd_d1 = '1'
                       else
             "ZZZZZZZZZZZZZZZZ";

end architecture single_port_mem_arch;
```

Single-port Memory

We introduce a new I/O port type; the "data_io" signal is declared as an "inout." This is VHDL's way of defining bi-directional signals. If "wr_en" is active, data driven onto the bi-directional data bus (data_io) from some source external to the FPGA is loaded into the "address" memory location. The data at this location is also registered into "data_out", but this goes into the bit-bucket.

If instead of "wr_en", "rd" is active, then along with the data in the memory being registered as "data_out", the active "rd" signal is also registered (i.e., delayed) as "rd_d1". During the following clock (when "rd_d1" is now active) the memory data being held in "data_out" is driven onto the external bi-directional data bus "data_io" by the combinatorial assignment statement below the process statement. Thus, for reads, the addressed memory data appears one clock after the read (rd) control is active. You may remember that this is how the dual-port structures worked as well. When reads are not occurring (i.e., when "rd_d1" is not active) the bus is tri-stated via "ZZZZZZZZZZZZZZZZ"—meaning "16 bits of high-impedance 'Z' ". Note that 'Z' is case-sensitive (it must be upper case). Note also that the STD_LOGIC_1164 library does not recognize the shortcut: X"ZZZZ".

Stretching out a string of Z's can get cumbersome for larger buses (imagine using this method for a wide, 256-bit bus), and fortunately, VHDL allows another shortcut method. Instead of all those Z's we can simply write:

```
(others => 'Z');
```

This works for other bit types as well, so, for example, instead of writing "000000", you could write (others => '0'). However, note that detailing the exact assignment communicates useful information—the width of the assigned vector bus.

This assignment statement—using tri-state internal buffers—is the key method to implement bi-directional buses. The following diagram illustrates the tri-state buffer as it would appear in our code.

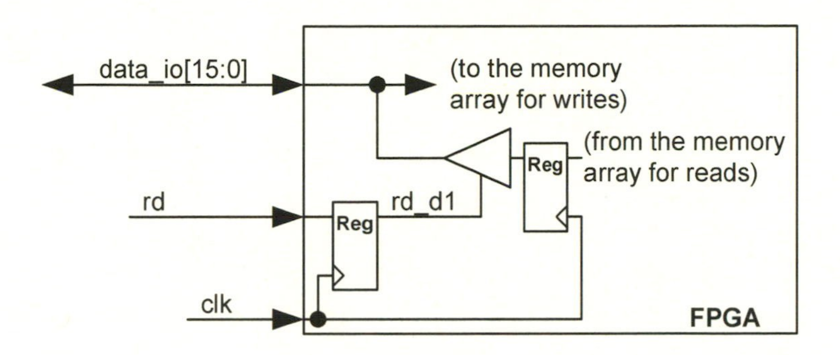

Tri-state buffer for bi-directional I/O

Tri-state interfaces are very common as external ports of FPGAs, and virtually all FPGA support them on external pins. Whether they are available as internal resources, however, depends on the vendor. E.g., Xilinx generally includes tri-state buffers in their FPGAs, but Altera does not. The Altera synthesis tools will accept the tri-state structure in the VHDL code, but will then implement the operation via a multiplexing method. The operation is the same, but can affect the routing timing (usually an issue only for designs with very fast clock speeds).

Managing Clocks

Synchronous design is synonymous with clocked operation, and virtually all non-trivial FPGA designs use one, and often multiple, clocks. It is difficult to overstate the importance of ensuring sound, precise clocking. For large, complex printed circuit board designs, this is often a dedicated development sub-system—a design specialization. Fortunately, the FPGA manufacturers have invested commensurate effort in developing reliable integrated clocking resources. Their engineers have developed a sophisticated clock generation, management, and distribution sub-system for you.

The clocking resources in FPGAs can be grouped into two categories: 1) clock distribution, and 2) clock synthesis. We have now encountered two uses of the word "synthesis," but whereas our first instance pertains to the formal definition of the word, whereby the VHDL code synthesis software "combines components to form a connected whole," clock synthesis, as we shall see, is more a process of creating modified versions of something (in this case, from a source clock).

The first category of clocking resource—distribution—consists of specialized FPGA buffers and routing facilities. Clock buffers are essentially current amplifiers powerful enough to drive a clock into the multitude of loads at far-flung locations with enough umph to ensure that the clock edge can arrive at each destination with minimum delay (and all at the same time, i.e., with no skew). In order to achieve this, the routing paths along the way must also be robust enough not to impose a load, meaning that they need to have sufficient metal. To this end, FPGAs have routing dedicated to clocks.

Accessing these special clock buffers (often called global buffers) and associated robust routing structures can be achieved in VHDL code by instantiating the clock buffer directly. Since the robust low-skew routing is driven directly by the buffer, it comes along for free. The following diagram shows a Xilinx clock buffer (BUFG), but each FPGA vendor has its own version. For example, the predominant Altera clock buffer is called "GCLK" (accessed via Altera's "global" primitive).

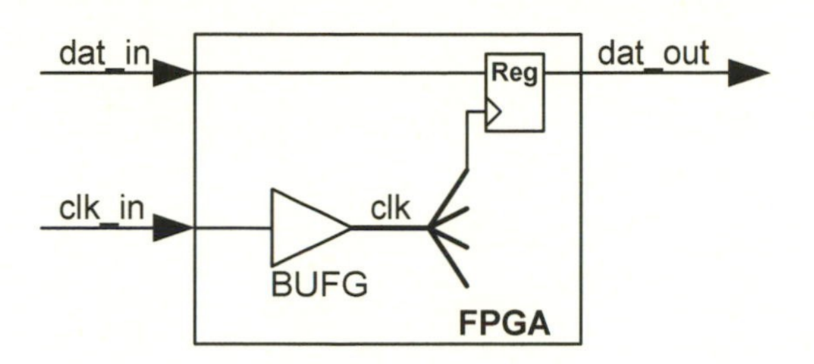

Clock Buffer

The following code shows the clock buffer instantiation, which looks like the module instantiations we saw earlier, because, of course, this is exactly what it is. The "BUFG" clock buffer is a vendor primitive, and is interpreted by the synthesis software as a black box (recall that the synthesis software simply passes these down to the vendor compiler, which presumably knows what they are). We recognize that once we begin using vendor-specific primitives, we are dedicating our code to that vendor.

```
-- ----------------------------------------------------
-- Header information
-- ----------------------------------------------------
library IEEE;
use IEEE.STD_LOGIC_1164.all;

entity clock_buffer is
  port (
         -- Inputs
         reset    : in  std_logic;
         clk_in   : in  std_logic;
         dat_in   : in  std_logic;
         -- Outputs
         dat_out  : out std_logic
       );
end entity clock_buffer;

architecture clock_buffer_arch of clock_buffer is
```

```
   signal clk   : std_logic;

   component BUFG
      port   (    I   : in  std_logic;
                  O   : out std_logic
             );
   end component;

begin

   --------------- Design implementation --------

   -- clock buffer instantiation
   clock_buf : BUFG
      port map
             (    I   => clk_in,
                  O   => clk
             );

   Reg_Proc: process (clk)
   begin
      if (reset = '1') then
         dat_out <= '0';
      elsif rising_edge(clk) then
         dat_out <= dat_in;
      end if;
   end process;

end architecture clock_buffer_arch;
```

Clock Buffer

This example uses an external clock input, but it is often possible to drive internally sourced clocks through clock buffers as well. One example is when receiving a high-speed serial interface (e.g., Gigabit Ethernet), where the Serdes IP core recovers the line clock, which must then be used for portions of the internal operation.

Sometimes the FPGA will have special dedicated clock inputs that connect to internal clock buffers directly, further reducing delay and skew. For example, most Xilinx FPGAs have dedicated clock inputs that are labeled as “GCLK” (making it a bit confusing when comparing to Altera devices, since they use the label for their clock buffers, and call their dedicated clock inputs simply “CLK”).

Since dedicated clock inputs are directly connected to internal clock buffers, there is no need to instantiate the clock buffer in the VHDL code (although it doesn't hurt). Further, in order to even use a global clock buffer, you might be required to bring the clock in on one of these special clock inputs. There's no getting around a careful look at the documentation regarding clocking requirements for the specific FPGA you intend to use.

Many newer synthesis tools will attempt to recognize clock signals that could do with a clock buffer and will automatically insert them for you (again, it doesn't hurt, and can only help, to make a direct instantiation).

A last word about clock distribution: newer, large FPGAs include increasingly complex clock routing and buffering resources. Particularly, due to the vast size and enormous quantity of potential loads, many large FPGAs include clocking subsections. These "regions" (often a quadrant of the die) host their own dedicated buffers and routes, where delay and skew can be reduced below what is possible for the global clocks (which are still available) that reach across the entire device. Some devices even include an even smaller sub-section. Often called "local clocks," these sub-areas are usually located along the periphery of the die and are associated with time-critical external interfaces.

The downside to this clocking sophistication is that when using these regional and local clocks, you introduce inherent partitioning to your design. You now have to be careful that all the logic associated with one of these sub-clocks can fit within the resources available in the sub-area, and more problematic, that all the logic can actually be *placed* by the complier in the sub-area. Conflicts arise, for example, when a signal that should be part of this sub-area is fed from or drives an external pin that is located in a different sub-area.

So far, we have looked at clock distribution that is sourced directly from an external clock. This is a common application, particularly where a single clock suffices for the logic operation, and the speeds are moderate enough that external signals can be clocked into and out of the FPGA with sufficient setup and hold times—up to perhaps 200 MHz. When the clocking structure and/or speeds extend beyond this, most FPGAs provide integrated PLL (Phase-Locked Loop) and/or DLL (Delay-Locked Loop) blocks that provide the resources needed for clock synthesis. PLL/DLLs provide the following functions in their role as the clock synthesis foundation, which we'll get to in turn:

- o phase alignment;
- o phased clock sets;
- o frequency multiplication.

We start with the DLLs, the simpler of the two synthesis functions. The delay in the diagram below is just that, except that it consists of a series of precise delay elements, from which the propagating clock signal can be tapped as "clk." The phase detector compares the phases (relative edges) at the input and output of the delay, and can select the delay tap that creates the desired phase offset. Thus, for example, we could choose a slightly negative phase offset (i.e., something less than 360 degrees) so that "clk" is effectively moved back in time. Then it could incur propagation delay in the FPGA and be back to approximately where it was coming in as "clk_in." The clock edges at the FPGA's internal registers would be (approximately) synchronized with those on the circuit board.

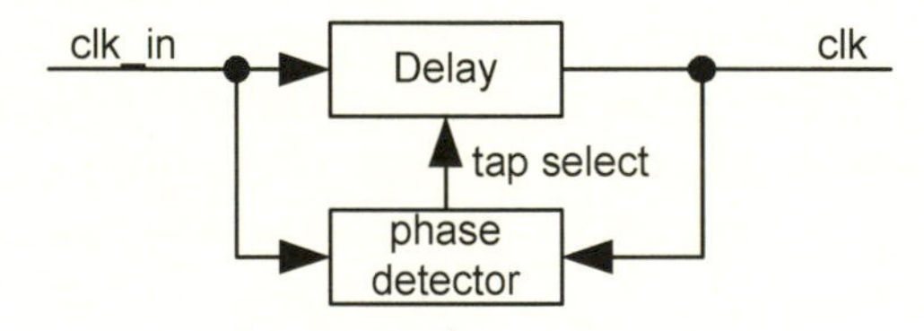

Simple DLL

But we can do better than this. Using the feedback path, we can arrange for the locked loop to automatically compensate for the internal propagation delays. If the phase detector in the following diagram were set to find a zero-degree phase difference, then it would select a delay tap accordingly. No matter how much delay is introduced between the delay and "clk," the internal clock would always be precisely in phase with the input clock (to within the quantum margins of the taps).

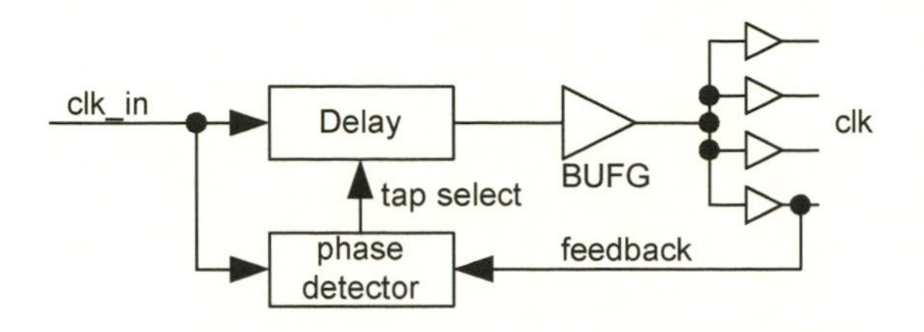

Propagation Compensated DLL

Thus, we have achieved the first point above: phase alignment.

Now imagine that we have multiple delay/phase detector sets. Suppose that the first is configured to select a tap to achieve phase alignment as described above, but the rest are slaved to the first, whereby each produces a version of "clk" that has a fixed (and convenient) phase offset—say, 90, 180, and 270 degrees. This is exactly what we often need in very high-speed designs—DDR and QDR memory interfaces, for example.

That knocks off the second point: phased clock sets.

We've dealt so far only with DLLs, and it's time to introduce the PLLs. The results are similar, but the means are radically different. You are probably already familiar with PLLs, as they have been a mainstay of electronics for nearly a century. The following diagram shows the delay unit of the DLL replaced with a voltage-controlled oscillator (VCO). Now, though, instead of selecting a delay tap, the phase detector develops a voltage (called an error signal) based on the phase difference. This voltage is arranged to provide negative feedback to the VCO—the phase offset moves the frequency of the VCO in the direction to bring the phase back to the desired position. If the phase detector is set to zero-phase offset, then you can see that this diagram functions the same as the previous DLL.

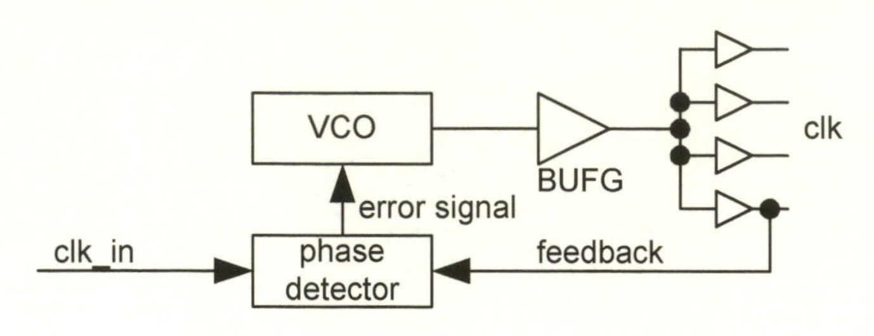

Propagation Compensated PLL

Since the DLL and PLL versions operate similarly, we will collect them together as a generic "Clock Generator" block and move on to talk about how internal clocks can be generated that have different frequencies than (but are still synchronized to) the original source clock. Frequency synthesis in FPGAs is accomplished in two steps: first, the frequency of the input source clock is multiplied up by some multiple amount (e.g., by 2, 3, 4, etc.), and then this higher frequency clock is divided back down by some other value. Although the up-multiplier is limited to integer numbers, the down-divider can typically also include half-values (e.g., 1.5, 2.0, 2.5, etc.). Thus, if we start with 10 MHz, and would like an internal clock of, say, 33.33 MHz, we could multiply up by ten, and then back down by three.

The following diagram shows how this is accomplished.

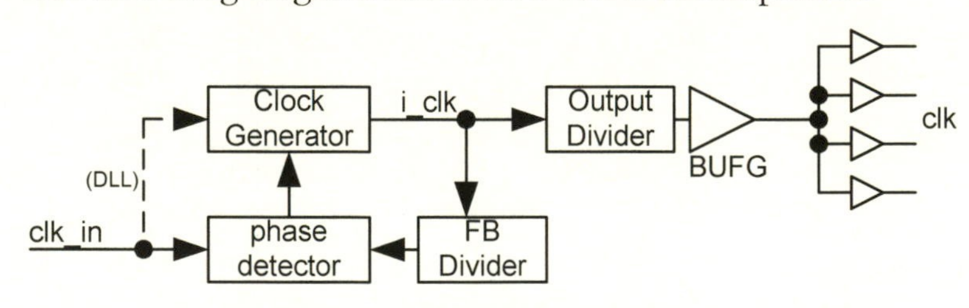

Frequency Synthesis

Since the phase detector wants to match the feedback clock to the input source clock, it must instruct the Clock Generator to create a higher frequency so that the FB Divider can reduce it back to that of the input source. (We haven't discussed how a tapped delay line can create outputs that are higher frequencies of the input, and we won't; you'll just have to take it on faith that this is so, as long as the desired frequency is an integer multiple of the source). The output of the Clock Generator is the intermediate up-multiplied clock mentioned above, labeled "i_clk" in the diagram. You can see that the multiplier value that is applied to the input source clock is simply the divider amount of the FB Divider. The Output Divider is just another divider that then reduces "i_clk" to the final desired frequency.

If we let "FB" stand for the FB Divider value, and "OD" stand for the Output Divider value, then the frequency of the final internal "clk" signal is:

clk frequency = (clk_in frequency) x (FB/OD)

The final step is now to mate the delay compensation of the earlier section with the frequency synthesis. In the following diagram, we've broken the path between the intermediate "i_clk" signal and carried it out through the FPGA clocking resources before presenting it to the FB Divider. As we saw earlier, this forces the "feedback" signal to be phase-aligned with the input "clk_in".

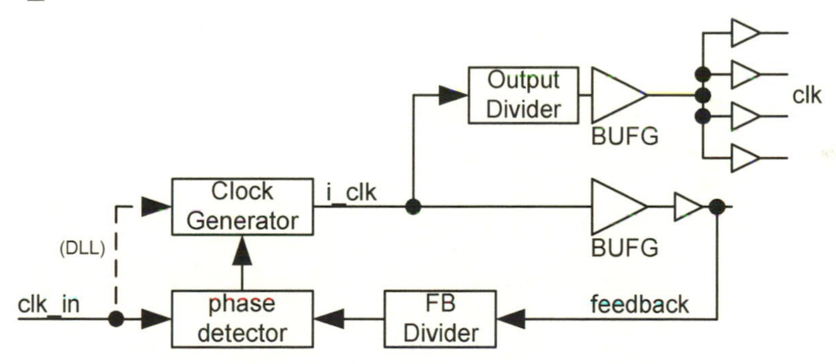

Frequency Synthesis w/ Delay Compensation

It is up to you, the designer, to make sure that the BUFG and routing paths associated with "feedback" match as closely as possible those associated with the main "clk" signal (the compiler software can often help with this via matched delays). The closer they match, the closer "clk" will be phase-aligned with the input "clk_in". We note that the FB Divider block will introduce some amount of delay, which offhand we might think would mess up the works, but it tends to be balanced by the Output Divider. The following timing diagram illustrates this.

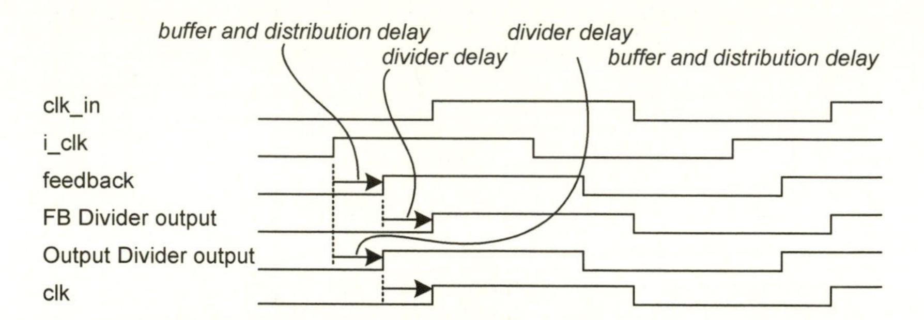

Frequency Synthesis Delay Compensation Timing

Note that "clk_in" and "clk" line up. This of course was the whole point. The output of the FP Divider also occurs coincident with "clk_in", and this is automatically a result of configuring a zero phase offset in the phase detector. Finally, note that "i_clk" is first in the pack, occurring far "before" the input clock "clk_in". This is magic of phase-locked loops.

Before we leave the subject of FPGA clocking, we'll compare DLLs and PLLs.

	DLL	PLL
jitter	The digital nature of DLLs results in some amount of small impulse-type jitter. This is rarely a problem with the internal digital logic, but can pose a problem for external interfaces that limit allowable jitter, such as communications links.	The analog nature of PLLs, on the other hand, exhibit much less jitter, and in some cases, a PLL might be inserted prior to a DLL for the exclusive purpose of reducing input jitter.
phase shift	Because of the same	PLLs offer some degree

	digital nature, DLLs generally have superior phase shifting capabilities, with outputs programmable to phase accuracies of just a few percent. Additionally, the phase shifts can often be programmed dynamically, meaning the FPGA logic can set them. Sometimes, even duty-cycles can be configured.	of phase-shifting, however, usually only in more general categories (e.g., phase quadrants). Also the phase shifts cannot (yet) be dynamically selected.
operating frequency	DLLs can operate at frequencies that approach the practical limits of the internal FPGA logic, but there are some cases where their ceiling is a limitation. More bothersome, they tend to operate in ranges (e.g., low, medium, and high), which need to be configured prior to compiling (and are therefore fixed).	PLLs are able to operate at higher frequencies for those special cases.
lock time	can be long	relatively short

We didn't introduce very much VHDL code in this chapter, but since it would be impossible to even begin many FPGA designs without an understanding of clocking methods, we might consider the material as a required entry ticket.

I/O Flavors

This is another chapter with very little actual VHDL code, but also another chapter that's hard to ignore once you start coding an actual design. Long gone are the days when digital circuits were entirely TTL, and the only interface question was whether the DIP chip was "AS" or "ALS" ("Advanced Schottky" or "Advanced Low-power Schottky"). With the emphasis now on high-speed operation, a large part of the circuit board design often comes down to a process of careful coordination of specialized interface signals—making sure the I/O signals of the integrated circuits are compatible. FPGAs have a tally-ho leg-up here, since not only do most host a wide selection of interface options, but they are configurable on a pin-by-pin basis (or at least pin group), making them the consummately flexible partner in the circuit board puzzle. In this chapter we'll review the general categories and types of interface options available.

Signal interfacing has evolved into a vast menagerie of standardized forms—LVCMOS(3.3V, 2.5V, 1.8V, etc.), LVDS, HSTL, LVPECL, SSTL(3, 2, 18, etc.), etc., etc.. Among the parameters defined for each are:

o voltage levels;

o slew rate;

o switching thresholds;

o differential pair versus single-ended;

o termination;

o drive impedance.

Fortunately, most current FPGAs allow some amount of control over each of these. Additionally, many vendors also provide some degree of control over additional I/O attributes, such as:

o inserted delay;

o drive strength;
o pullup/pulldown/keepers;
o tri-state drive.

These various parameters are defined via three methods in the design of the FPGA: 1) instantiating special I/O primitives in the VHDL code, 2) voltages applied externally to dedicated pins, and 3) design constraints.

We haven't talked about design constraints yet. Every FPGA design consists of two parts: the design code (VHDL or verilog), and a list of constraints. All of these—code and constraints—consist of text files. These constraints comprise essentially everything needed to build an operating FPGA that isn't included directly in the code itself. The constraints are entirely unique to the particular FPGA vendor, and many to the particular device itself, right down to the exact device package. The most common type of constraint is the pin definition—information associating an external device pin to an I/O signal. A 16-bit bus will have 16 different pin constraints. Every design has pin constraints as a minimum, but beyond these, there are many, many types of information that can be included. One major class is timing constraints, whereby you can define minimum and/or maximum propagation paths, I/O setup and hold, and minimum clock speeds. Discussions of these are well beyond the scope of this book, and are best handled via the vendor's documentation anyway. The third major class of constraints is the I/O definitions, which brings us back to these parameters.

We'll take a look at each of these and see how they are used and defined.

output voltage levels

Interface signal levels can range from 3.3 Volts down to less than a Volt. External input pins define the drive voltage. The FPGA designer must coordinate with the circuit board design to make sure the proper voltage is used for a desired standard. Note that I/O pins are grouped together in banks, where all I/O pins in the same bank share the same external drive voltage pin. Thus, all the signals connecting to a bank must share the same signal voltage level. We guarantee that this limitation will ultimately cause you much grief.

slew rate

Slew rate is typically categorized as simply "slow" or "fast". This parameter is defined, per pin, in the constraint file.

switching thresholds

Input voltage thresholds are for the most part defined via constraints. Each pin has its own constraint line, where the actual I/O standard is declared (one that is supported by the vendor). The constraint format is defined in the FPGA vendor's documentation.

Some I/O standards (those that define pseudo-differential input amplifiers) require a reference voltage provided by an external pin similar to that which establishes the output drive voltage.

differential pair versus single-ended

Differential pairs are defined by two means, both required. First, the two halves of a differential pair must be paired to proper FPGA I/O pins. The FPGA device hosts pin pairs that can either be used as one differential pair, or two single-ended signals. If used as a differential pair, these two pins further must be mated correctly with the positive and negative halves of the differential pair (if not, the logic polarity of the signal is reversed). Second, a differential receiver/driver black box primitive is instantiated in the code.

Single-ended signals are the default and need no definition.

Note that in addition to assigning the differential pair to proper pin pairs and instantiating a differential driver/receiver black box, a constraint may be additionally needed if the differential signal is to adhere to a specific I/O standard.

source impedance / termination

The very resourceful FPGA vendor engineers have developed means to digitally mimic source (i.e. drive impedance) and termination resistors. When used, these virtual resistors eliminate the physical resistors normally placed on the circuit board near the FPGA I/O pin. This has distinct advantages, particularly with ever-higher speeds and ever-denser FPGA packaging. With very dense ball-grid packaging, the resulting cluster of termination resistors means that many resistors simply cannot be located optimally close, resulting in high-speed stub effects.

The internal virtual FPGA termination resistors can be either in series or parallel. The impedance value (drive source for outputs, and termination for receivers) is set using two external resistors: one tied up to the same pin that defines the output drive voltage, and the other tied to ground. The value of these resistors (they have the same value) determine the internal virtual impedance for the entire bank as described above for output voltage levels.

Additionally, special I/O buffer black box primitives are instantiated in the VHDL code. These may be dedicated primitives per resistor configuration, or the standard I/O primitive with additional attributes included—often simply the I/O standard being implemented. In all cases, as with other black boxes, these primitives will be unique to the FPGA vendor.

A common example is a differential receiver, where a virtual differential 100 Ohm termination is added.

inserted delay

Another tool developed by the FPGA vendors is insertable delays for both inputs and outputs. These are used to adjust setup and hold times, and are essentially the same as the external delay lines used since the beginning of digital design in the seventies. The signal passes through a delay path, and the output is selected from one of a series of taps. The tap selection (i.e., the delay incurred) can be fixed, or dynamically controlled. The latter is generally used when fine tuning very high-speed ports.

These artificial delays are invoked via instantiated black box primitives in the VHDL code.

drive strength

The current drive of outputs can be controlled to some extent. The drive capability can be limited, often in increments of 2 mA; thus you can set the drive strength at 2 mA, 4 mA, 6 mA, etc.. In fact, the drive strength isn't so much limited, as enabled (how many drive transistors are used), so the actual maximum current available will vary somewhat.

Limiting the drive current is often useful in controlling transmission effects; limiting drive current can dampen the energy that might otherwise go into reflections. The downside is that too-low drive strength can result in too-slow transitions. Drive strength often goes hand-in-hand with the slew-rate control.

Note that the FPGA die can handle only so much power locally at the I/O areas, and there may be a limit to how many high-drive outputs are defined in any one group.

The drive strength is normally defined in the constraint file.

tri-state drive

Tri-state outputs were covered above in the Memories section, but here we note that, in addition to the VHDL-inferred method discussed there, these can also be invoked directly with vendor-specific black box primitives.

pullup / pulldown / keepers

These pullups and pulldowns are different from the virtual source/termination resistors discussed above in that they are actual resistors, albeit weak (high-value). They are not meant for termination, but rather to maintain an undriven input at either a high or low logic level. Pullups and pulldowns can also be added to tri-state outputs, again keeping the signal at a known level when the tri-state buffer is disabled (but allowing other external tri-state drivers to override the weak resistor).

Additionally, "keepers" can be added to tri-state outputs. These are nifty little circuits that hold the output weakly at whatever level was present when the tri-state driver was disabled. Handily, they work even when it's an external tri-state driver that has retired its drive. Since tri-state outputs are half of a bi-directional port, a keeper would in this case be holding the last driven level also for internal logic of the FPGA.

All of these weak input/output level-maintaining features are invoked by either instantiating black box primitives in the VHDL code, or with attributes in the constraint file.

Before leaving the subject of special I/O, we will look briefly at a functional block that is a type of I/O, but also a whole complex sub-design of its own. This is the SERDES, which stands for SERializer-DESerializer, and like the memory structures earlier, is included in many FPGAs as a pre-designed section of circuitry separate from the programmable logic fabric. SERDES blocks allow relatively easy access to high-speed serial interfaces that otherwise might not be implementable in the FPGA at all.

At their core they are, as their name implies, blocks that convert incoming serial streams into parallel words, and vice-versa. But they are more than simple shift registers. The simplest ones facilitate DDR (dual data rate) and bit-slip operation (useful when the serial stream includes a framing pattern that must be located). The complex SERDES available in the larger FPGAs perform PLL-based clock recovery from the serial stream, and link layer functions such as 8B/10B symbol encoding/decoding, comma detection and word alignment, and beacon signaling. Additionally, they include FIFOs for rate smoothing and PRBS generators/checkers for testing. Coupled with IP cores, they allow FPGAs to host such high-bandwidth serial interfaces as PCI Express, 10 Gigabit Ethernet, and SONET high-rate links. These sophisticated blocks perform as an auxiliary function in FPGAs what used to require an entire dedicated ASIC.

A Taste of Simulation

VHDL simulation is another subject that would require an entire (thick) book of its own to cover comprehensively. We will, however, take a passing look at how you can at least get started with simple approaches, perhaps useful for initial syntax checking and testing example code.

Simulation of VHDL code consists of creating even more VHDL code that exercises and monitors the code to be tested. This test-only code is called a testbench, and as the name evokes, is a virtual platform upon which your design rests and where virtual wires are connected to your I/O for stimulation and response. All of this is done under the control and execution of the hosting simulation software tool. To repeat, in order to simulate your design, you need some sort of simulation software tool. Luckily, "beginner" versions of popular simulation software are often available free from the FPGA vendors.

Firstly, we need some sample code to simulate. The following diagram shows a simple function, whereby if enabled, a series of 8-bit words are checked as to whether any two consecutive values are the same, and if found, are tallied. Note that the last word of a sequence block is held in the register and compared with the first word of the next series.

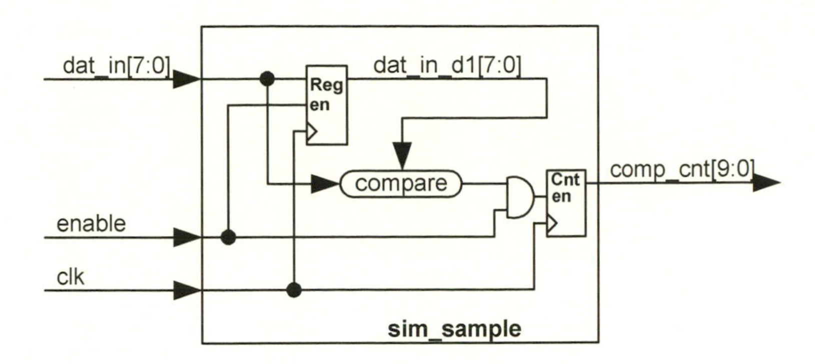

Sample Simulation Design

And here's the code.

```
-- ---------------------------------------------------
-- Header information
-- ---------------------------------------------------
library IEEE;
use IEEE.STD_LOGIC_1164.all;
use IEEE.NUMERIC_STD.all;

entity sim_sample is
  port (
         -- Inputs
         clk          : in  std_logic;
         rst          : in  std_logic;
         --
         dat_in       : in  std_logic_vector(7 downto 0);
         enable       : in  std_logic;

         -- Outputs
         comp_cnt     : out std_logic_vector(9 downto 0)
       );
end entity sim_sample;

architecture sim_sample_arch of sim_sample is

   signal dat_in_d1       : std_logic_vector(7 downto 0);
   signal comp_cnt_lcl    : unsigned(9 downto 0);

begin

   Sim_Sample_Proc: process (clk, rst)
   begin
      if (rst = '1') then
```

```
         dat_in_d1    <= X"00";
         comp_cnt_lcl <= "00" & X"00";
      elsif rising_edge(clk) then
         if (enable = '1') then

            dat_in_d1 <= dat_in;

            if (dat_in_d1 = dat_in) then
               comp_cnt_lcl <= comp_cnt_lcl + 1;
            end if;

         end if;

      end if;
   end process;

   comp_cnt <= std_logic_vector(comp_cnt_lcl);

end architecture sim_sample_arch;
```

Sample Simulation Design

All the aspects of this code should be familiar from previous examples, e.g., using an unsigned type for the counter, and including the associated NUMERIC_STD library.

Now we need a testbench (VHDL code) to test our design. What we require is some way to feed a series of 8-bit values to our "sim_sample" module along with an enable signal, and then check to make sure the tallied count is incrementing correctly.

The following diagram shows the pieces.

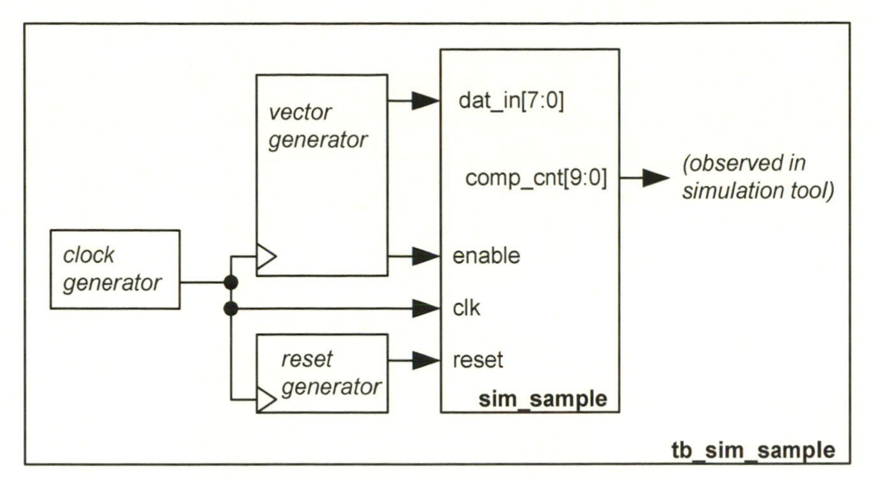

Testbench Using Embedded Vectors

We'll start with the simplest possible testbench.

```
-- -----------------------------------------------------
-- Simple Testbench Using Embedded, Explicit Vectors
-- -----------------------------------------------------
library IEEE;
use IEEE.STD_LOGIC_1164.all;
use IEEE.NUMERIC_STD.all;

entity tb_sim_sample_1 is
end entity tb_sim_sample_1;

architecture Behavioral of tb_sim_sample_1 is

   component sim_sample
     port (
           -- Inputs
           clk          : in  std_logic;
           rst          : in  std_logic;
           --
           dat_in       : in  std_logic_vector(7 downto 0);
           enable       : in  std_logic;

           -- Outputs
           comp_cnt     : out std_logic_vector(9 downto 0)
          );
   end component;

   constant HALF_PERIOD  : time := 5 ns; -- 100MHz = 10ns
```

```
   -- module-under-test inputs
   signal clk           : std_logic;
   signal rst           : std_logic;
   signal data_val      : std_logic_vector(7 downto 0);
   signal en            : std_logic;

   -- module-under-test outputs
   signal comp_cnt      : std_logic_vector(9 downto 0);

begin

   -- module under test

   MUT: sim_sample
   port map
     (
       -- Inputs
       clk        => clk,
       rst        => rst,
       --
       dat_in     => data_val,
       enable     => en,

       -- Outputs
       comp_cnt   => comp_cnt
     );

   -----------------------------------------------------
   ------  Clock Generator
   -----------------------------------------------------

   clk <= '0' after HALF_PERIOD when clk = '1' else
          '1' after HALF_PERIOD;

   -----------------------------------------------------
   ------  Reset Generator
   -----------------------------------------------------

   Reset_Gen : process
   begin
     -- generate reset
     for i in 1 to 5 loop
        if (i < 4) then
           rst <= '1';
        else
           rst <= '0';
        end if;
        wait until falling_edge(clk);
     end loop;
     --
     -- de-activate this process
```

```
     wait on rst;
   end process Reset_Gen;

   -----------------------------------------------------
   ------  Vector Generator
   -----------------------------------------------------

   Vector_Generate_explicit: process

   begin

     data_val <= X"00";
     en       <= '0';

     wait until falling_edge(rst);

     for j in 1 to 3 loop
        wait until falling_edge(clk);
     end loop;

     en <= '1';

     wait until falling_edge(clk);
     data_val <= X"01";
     wait until falling_edge(clk);
     data_val <= X"20";
     wait until falling_edge(clk);
     data_val <= X"21";
     wait until falling_edge(clk);
     data_val <= X"21";
     wait until falling_edge(clk);
     data_val <= X"33";
     wait until falling_edge(clk);
     data_val <= X"56";
     wait until falling_edge(clk);
     data_val <= X"56";
     wait until falling_edge(clk);
     data_val <= X"33";
     wait until falling_edge(clk);

     en <= '0';

     -- de-activate this process
     wait on rst;

   end process Vector_Generate_explicit;

end architecture Behavioral;
```

Testbench Using Embedded, Explicit Vectors

For a simplest of testbenches, there's still a lot of new VHDL material to learn. We start at the very beginning with the entity declaration "tb_sim_sample_1". We include no port list, since the testbench has no signals entering or leaving—it comprises the entire simulation universe. We proceed directly to the architecture, where we find the component declaration for our module-under-test (sim_sample). This is just a lower-level hierarchical module that will be instantiated, the same as those covered in the module design chapter. Skip over the constant declaration for now, but note that a "constant" is just that—a fixed value as assigned via ":=". Following that, we have the signal declarations, and they consist of two categories: signals that are inputs to the module to be simulated, and signals that are outputs from the module. The input signals will be generated and driven by the testbench, while the module outputs are simply monitored for correct operation. As we begin the body of our architecture, we come immediately to the instantiation of our sample module—the module to be simulated (although it could be placed anywhere in the architecture body).

Finally we get to some actual simulation activity. The first signal we'll generate as part of the simulation is the clock ("clk"). The basic structure should look familiar, as it is simply the "when-else" statement we learned in the In and Out chapter early on. Think of it this way:

> when "clk" is high, it goes low after a delay, else
> (when it's low) "clk" goes high after a delay.

You can see that the "delay" is equal to half the period of the resulting clock (thus the label "half_delay"). We introduce a new VHDL concept, time. When creating synthesizable logic, the aspect of time is usually not a factor; a clock—either provided externally, or synthesized via internal PLLs—serves to advance the gears of our logical watch ahead at a steady pace (an exception is when we need to specifically configure internal delays, but this is most often done via tool-specific configuration files, either directly, or via setup and hold requirements). But in simulation, the testbench must create and control this fourth dimension. Fundamentally, this may be by generating the logic-ratcheting clock, but also could be emulating real-world situations spanning milliseconds, or more.

So, the "after" clause dictates exactly what the word implies: an action occurs "after" a prescribed delay. The constant "half_period" was declared with the new type "time", and assigned a value of five nano-seconds. VHDL recognizes "ns", "us" (micro-seconds), "ms" (milliseconds), etc.. In the following statement, the assignment of the logical AND to "sig_out" is delayed by three nanoseconds, defining a prescribed internal FPGA delay (however, as I indicated, this sort of thing is usually handled within configuration files used by the synthesis tool):

```
sig_out <= (gate_control AND sig_in) AFTER 3 ns;
```

The next signal that the testbench generates is the reset signal "rst", which in this testbench will go active just one time at the beginning of operation (e.g., after power-up) for a predetermined duration, which for this example will be just three clocks. This is done with a "for loop," something similar with which you may have already encountered in software. The loop—i.e., the statements between the "for" line and the "end loop" line—is executed a number of times, as defined by values in the "for" line. Each time through the loop, the integer "i" is incremented, starting with the defined value of one, and ending with the defined value of five. So in this case, the statements inside the for-loop will execute five times. As long as "i" is less than four (the first three passes through the loop), the "rst" signal will remain active, but will then go inactive after that. At the end of the loop we come to a "wait until" statement, which does just what it says, simulation execution pauses (here) until the next falling edge of the clock. Thus, the "wait until" clause effects the same sort of clocked sequential operation as a clock-driven process (e.g., a register).

So, to recap, using the "for loop," we have generated a "rst" signal that goes active for three clocks, and then goes inactive. Once we exit the "for loop," the simulation comes to the "wait on" statement. Here, the simulation will pause until there is some change to the "rst" signal. However, at this point, the "rst" signal will no longer change, so the simulation will pause here indefinitely. This is exactly what we want, otherwise the process will repeat, over and over, generating a toggling "rst" signal. We note that although the simulation is paused within this process, other processes continue independently.

Notice that I used a falling edge of the clock to define the transitions of the "rst" signal. This is done in order to place the "rst" transitions away from the active rising edges of operation of the instantiated module under test. In actual operation, we count on natural propagation delays to delay transitions of one registered stage (e.g., outside the FPGA) to another (e.g., inside the FPGA), thus satisfying the target register's hold time requirement. I could have achieved this with a bunch of "after" time clauses on all the testbench-generated signals, but this method is straightforward and much less cluttered.

A word about "for loops" and synthesis: testbench operation in simulation tends to proceed from a fixed starting point through some progression for a finite period of time, and it is useful and appropriate to have structures such as controlled loops and "wait on" statements to define and control the linear sequence of operation. This is more akin to software than hardware. When synthesizing FPGA logic, however, the synthesis tool must somehow translate these statements into gates and registers. Although it is possible to use, for example, "for loops" in synthesis, I would recommend avoiding this until you are confident in predicting how the synthesis tool will react.

Back to our testbench, we leave the reset generator, and finally come to the generation of the actual stimulus vectors. Again, we note that although the statements proceed in sequence within each process, all the processes of the testbench operate in parallel and at the same time (concurrently). This process proceeds step-by-step from beginning to end, laying out a linear sequence of actions. We begin by establishing starting values for our two vectors (the "data_val" and "en" signals that we will feed to the module under test). The process then waits until the reset is complete, and then waits another three clocks via another "for loop" before taking action. Finally, three clocks after the reset is lifted, the "en" enable signal is activated, followed by eight different "data_val" values presented in successive clocks. Finally, on the next clock after the last stimulus value, the enable "en" is de-activated.

Here's what the simulation looks like as presented on a waveform viewer:

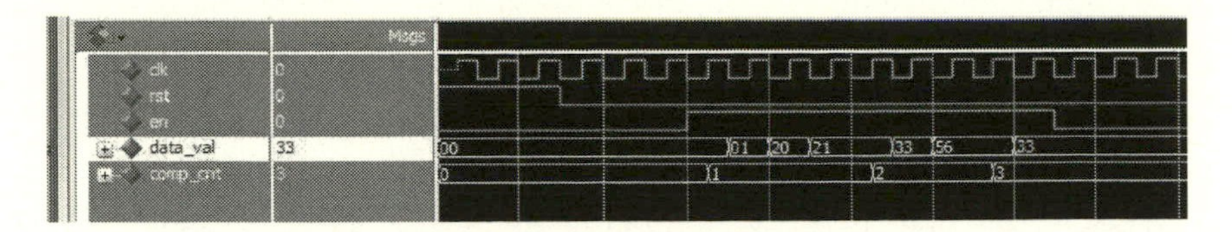

So, what have we done with this simulation? We set the clock running, reset the FPGA, and then fed eight input data samples. Looking at the values we fed, we see that there were two instances of repeating data words (hex 21 and hex 56), and so we expect the counter output, "com_cnt", to increment twice. Note that it increments immediately from zero to one, though; this is because both "dat_in_d1" and "dat_in" of sim_sample are initially zero (and thus are equal).

Alternatively, we could have programmed the testbench to itself recognize that the count has incremented and display the fact on our monitor. This could be done via the "$display" simulation directive, but we won't go further with that avenue here.

The previous testbench is fine for a limited amount of data, but obviously becomes quickly cumbersome as the amount increases to practical quantities (practical quantities for a practical design, that is—eight samples is okay for our simple sample design). The following testbench generates stimulus data vector values automatically using semi-random numbers. It has the advantage that we can generate as many vectors as we like by simply changing a parameter value.

```
-- ------------------------------------------------------
-- Simple Testbench Using Embedded, Automatic Vectors
-- ------------------------------------------------------
library IEEE;
use IEEE.STD_LOGIC_1164.all;
use IEEE.NUMERIC_STD.all;

entity tb_sim_sample_2 is
end entity tb_sim_sample_2;

architecture Behavioral of tb_sim_sample_2 is

   component sim_sample
     port (
            -- Inputs
            clk         : in  std_logic;
            rst         : in  std_logic;
```

```
        --
        dat_in      : in  std_logic_vector(7 downto 0);
        enable      : in  std_logic;

        -- Outputs
        comp_cnt    : out std_logic_vector(9 downto 0)
       );
   end component;

   constant HALF_PERIOD   : time := 5 ns;   -- 100MHz = 10ns
   constant QUANT_VECTORS : integer := 30; -- number of vectors
   -- semi-random seed
   constant SEED  : unsigned(5 downto 0) := "100111";

   -- module-under-test inputs
   signal clk           : std_logic;
   signal rst           : std_logic;
   signal data_val      : std_logic_vector(7 downto 0);
   signal en            : std_logic;

   -- module-under-test outputs
   signal comp_cnt      : std_logic_vector(9 downto 0);

begin

   -- module under test

   MUT: sim_sample
   port map
     (
       -- Inputs
       clk         => clk,
       rst         => rst,
       --
       dat_in      => data_val,
       enable      => en,

       -- Outputs
       comp_cnt    => comp_cnt
     );

   ----------------------------------------------------
   ------  Clock Generator
   ----------------------------------------------------

   clk <= '0' after HALF_PERIOD when clk = '1' else
          '1' after HALF_PERIOD;

   ----------------------------------------------------
   ------  Reset Generator
   ----------------------------------------------------

   Reset_Gen : process
   begin
     -- generate reset
     for i in 1 to 5 loop
        if (i < 4) then
           rst <= '1';
        else
```

```
         rst <= '0';
      end if;
      wait until falling_edge(clk);
    end loop;
    --
    -- de-activate this process
    wait on rst;
  end process Reset_Gen;

  ---------------------------------------------------
  ------  Vector Generator
  ---------------------------------------------------

  Vector_Generate_Implicit: process

     variable semi_random : unsigned(5 downto 0) := "101010";
     variable data_val_un : unsigned(7 downto 0) := X"00";

  begin

    data_val <= X"00";
    en       <= '0';

    wait until falling_edge(rst);

    for j in 1 to 3 loop
       wait until falling_edge(clk);
    end loop;

    en <= '1';

    for i in 1 to QUANT_VECTORS loop

       semi_random := semi_random + SEED;

       if (semi_random(5 downto 4) /= "00") then
          data_val_un := data_val_un + 1;
       end if;

       data_val <= std_logic_vector(data_val_un);

       wait until falling_edge(clk);

    end loop;

    en <= '0';

    -- de-activate this process
    wait on rst;

  end process Vector_Generate_Implicit;

end architecture Behavioral;
```

Testbench Using Embedded, Automatic Vectors

Let's look at what's different from the previous testbench. First, we have a new constant called QUANT_VECTORS. As we'll see (and as you've guessed), this is a parameter that defines how many stimulus vectors we'll generate for the test run. We've also added a constant called SEED, and this will be explained later. Otherwise, the clock and reset generation are the same, and we move down to the Vector Generator. We see that I've added two variables, "semi_random" and "data_val_un". You probably remember that I recommended against using variables for the synthesized logic, but their use is fairly standard in testbenches, where we're naturally thinking in terms of sequential flow (which can cause unexpected results with variables if not careful otherwise). Note that both variables are declared as unsigned, since we will be performing arithmetic operations on them, and that they are both assigned initial values, using the same ":=" assignment operator we saw with constants.

We see that the sequence of fixed vector value assignments of the explicit testbench has been replaced here with a for-loop, which cycles a QUANT_VECTORS number of times. Each pass through the loop, "semi_random" is incremented by the constant SEED value. If you only look at, for example, bits 4 and 5, the resulting sequence of two-bit values will appear to be random (I call it "semi_random", since there are more comprehensive ways to generate nearly random—pseudo-random—numbers, but this simpler method is fine for our purposes). The "if" conditional statement that follows then increments the unsigned version of the "data_val" as long as the two-bit semi-random value is not "00". Thus, on average, one-out-of-four loop passes "data_val" will not be incremented, presenting a non-changing value to the sim_sample module under test (and hopefully causing our comparison counter to increment).

The following picture shows the resulting simulation result.

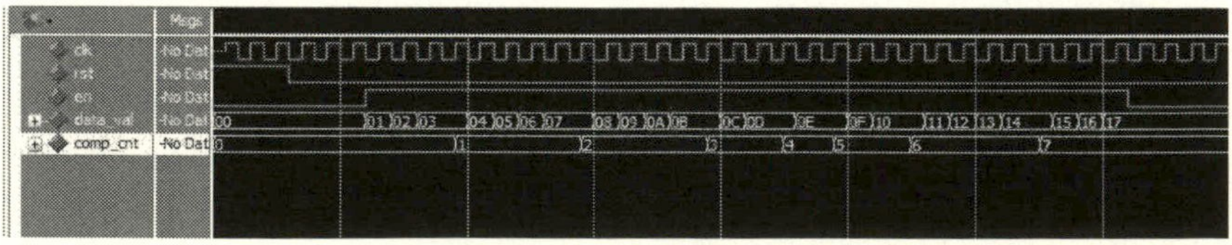

Although efficient and easily understood, this testbench does have the weakness that the stimulus vector values are always incrementing by one (or occasionally static). In some designs, this limitation could be limiting, foregoing some value transitions that might be important—values stepping from X"55" to X"AA", to take one example. In the opposite direction, we might need less randomness and even more control. One example is a local processor bus, where we are simulating bus protocol activity—perhaps a microprocessor on the host board filling a configuration memory inside the FPGA. For specific control over the stimulus values we might come right back to that long list of embedded specific stimulus values. But there is a better way to handle long lists of vectors, a flexible and powerful method of generating stimulus vectors, whereby the testbench reads the values from external files, files that we've filled with our test vectors. Further, the testbench could even confirm outputs from the design by comparing them against additional result-files.

This is where we could continue if this book were a thorough, dedicated treatise of simulation instead of a concise introduction to overall VHDL design.

The Rest for Reference

The best way to learn is to do, and in this case doing is designing. This has not been an exhaustive study by any measure, neither of all the fine points of VHDL, nor even of some major features, but by now you should at least have acquired a solid foundation to begin in earnest, learning more as you build, point-by-point, new knowledge from other sources.

You'll need tools, though. The two dominant FPGA vendors, Xilinx and Altera, provide free introductory packages that also include free introductory simulation software. The web packages are quite large, so be sure to check your computer's resources against the requirements listed on the vendor's website.

What follows is for reference. As you work to mold lines of code, or struggle to reverse-engineer an undocumented design, peruse these pages for tidbits to help. Most of the following are just hints, mere nods at some of the deeper features available with VHDL, but just knowing that something is possible is often essential as you can then reach out to other texts and references for more complete discussions.

Expressions

(Note that the shift operators won't work with std_logic_vector types, but they will with bit_vector types).

Concatenation &
X"6" & "1010" & X"2" = "011010100010"

Logical operators and, or, not, nand, nor, xor, xnor

Arithmetic	+, -, *, /
Relational	=, /=, <, >, <=, >=
Modulus	mod (X"A" mod X"3") = 1 (X"A" mod X"2") = 0 (X"A" mod X"4") = 2
Remainder	rem (same as mod if both operands are positive)
Absolute value	abs
shift left logical	sll ("111001" sll 1) = "110010" ("111001" sll 2) = "100100"
shift right logical	srl ("111001" srl 1) = "011100" ("111001" srl 2) = "001110"
shift left arithmetic	sla ("111001" sla 1) = "110011" ("111001" sla 2) = "100111"
shift right arithmetic	sra ("111001" sra 1) = "111100" ("111001" sra 2) = "111110"

Types

The signal types covered (or at least mentioned) in the body of this book included std_logic, std_logic_vector, unsigned, signed, integers, arrays, and homemade (labels we made up for the state machine). Here are some more:

bit and bit_vector: these are more general and have a broader application than their brothers, std and std_vector (we note that shift operations work on these but not std_logic). These are considered to be "unconstrained," meaning that their size can be left undefined until used. They are particularly useful when creating and using subprograms (functions and procedures);

boolean: holds the values of "true" or "false." This can be useful if, for example, the only use of the signal/variable is for conditional control. Thus, instead of:

```
if (signal_name = '1') then
```

when "signal_name" is declared as boolean, the same line could be simplified to:

```
if (signal_name) then
```

real: just like in mathematics, a real type can include fractional components of numbers, e.g., 5.426, or 1.24E3. This type has very limited application in everyday synthesized code;

file: this type is used for handling files. Used almost exclusively in simulation (versus synthesized logic), the "file" type allows stimulus vectors and simulation results to be accessed and stored in support files. Very powerful;

access: similar to a pointer in software. You would only ever (if ever) use this in a sophisticated simulation testbench;

subtype: simply a subset of another type;

record: a record is similar to an array, except that instead of a table of similar-sized and typed values, a record can hold entries of different sizes and types. This is particularly useful when connecting a multitude of signals up and/or down through a multi-layered hierarchy. You are essentially bundling the group of signals together into one neat label. Furthermore, the record declaration can be made just once in an associated package (described later), avoiding cluttering the various modules of the hierarchy. Here's an example record declaration:

```
TYPE io_pipe is
   RECORD
      enable      : std_logic;
      clear       : std_logic;
      data_in     : std_logic_vector(15 downto 0);
      data_out    : std_logic_vector(15 downto 0);
      address     : std_logic_vector(9 downto 0);
      done_flag   : std_logic;
   END_RECORD;
```

Generics

Generics are used to pass instance-specific information down into an entity, and are thus similar to "defines" in C and verilog. Some common types of information passed into an entity are bus widths, use-control (tailoring some specifics of the entity's operation on a per-instance basis), and simulation control (where, for example, you might need to bypass device-specific clock buffers, etc. for functional simulation, where they aren't really needed anyway). Note that in the last example, a single generic at the top-level module could be passed successively down into all the hierarchical modules, allowing the entire design to be configured for simulation versus synthesis with a single top-level change.

Generics must be static, i.e. have a fixed value, at compile time. So, you can't use a signal, for example, to assign to a generic. But you could use a constant, or another generic that has been passed down.

Generics are declared in a component declaration just before the port list, like so:

```
component my_next_module
   generic
     (
      -- true for simulation, false for compiling.
      Simulation_on : boolean := false;
      -- width of data bus
      bus_width     : integer := 8
```

```
      );
    port (
          data_bus : in  std_logic_vector(7 downto 0);
         (etc.)
```

Note that the value associated with the generic is not relevant here, since it will be re-established later in the component instantiation. The generics are then included in the component instantiation like so:

```
  my_next_module_inst : my_next_module
    generic map
      (
       Simulation_on : Simulation_on;
       bus_width     : 16
      );
    port (
          data_bus  => data_bus_in,
          (etc.)
```

Notice that I have assigned "Simulation_on" to the generic of the same name. This is because I'm passing this switch value down through the hierarchy. This is an example of a generic being assigned to another generic. Notice also that I've changed the "bus_width" to 16 (from the straw man 8 in the component declaration).

Finally, here's the generics in the lower-level instantiated module.

```
  entity my_next_module is
    generic
      (
       Simulation_on : boolean := false;
       bus_width     : integer := 8
      );
    port (
         data_bus : in std_logic_vector(bus_width-1
                                              downto 0);
```

We must understand that it doesn't matter to what assignments the generics have been made here—they will be overridden from above. In this case, "Simulation_on" will take on whatever value was passed from above by the same name, while "bus_width" will be the 16 we used in the component instantiation. Note how the "bus_width" generic is now used to size "data_bus".

Generate

The "generate" statement is generally used to instantiate a replicated group of component modules, for example memory blocks, or perhaps multiple identical communication I/O channels. Here's an example.

```
arbitrary_label : for i in 0 to 7 generate
    the_module_inst : the_module
       port map
        (
         clk        => clk,
         an_input   => x_array(i),
         an_output  => y_array(i)
        );
end generate;
```

Arrays are almost always used for some of the assignments, since we can index through them via the generate loop variable ("i"). Only those signals that have the same connection across all the replicated instantiations are not done with arrays (as "clk" in this example).

We should note that generics can also be used for conditional compiling, but since the conditional decision cannot be passed down from high-level modules, this feature has limited application (unlike verilog, where it can).

Functions

A function in VHDL is similar to those you may have encountered in other programming languages: a function can have one or more inputs, but there are no outputs, or rather, there is just one virtual output—the value returned by the function. Functions are declared and defined within a module, and can then only be used in that module, or they can be declared and defined within a package, and then can be used in any module that includes the package. Functions can include any statements that could be used in a process. Functions are called from an expression, and the returned value becomes part of that expression. There's no utility in creating a function that you use just once, unless your goal is to fatten your lines of code.

Following is an example of a function that finds and returns the location of the largest value within a specified number of elements of an array.

First we declare and define the function at the beginning of the architecture (the same place we declare signals and components):

```
architecture example_arch of example is

   FUNCTION
   largest_value
     (
      array_in   : my_array_type;
      amount     : integer
     ) RETURN integer is
     variable temp_max : std_logic_vector(7 downto 0);
     variable index    : integer;
   BEGIN
      temp_max := X"00";
      for i in 0 to amount loop
         if (array_in(i) > temp_max) then
           temp_max := array_in(i);
           index    := i;
         end if;
      end loop;
      RETURN index;
   END largest_value;
```

I'm using upper case for those labels that are reserved and required. The label "largest_value" is the name of the function, and the label we'll use later to call it. Like an entity, the function has input ports, here "array_in" (the array where we'll search for the largest value) and "amount" (how deep into the array to look). The "my_array_type" is a unique array type that would have been elsewhere declared for use in this entity. The "RETURN" that immediately follows declares the type of value that will be returned when the function completes.

Next we declare the local variables we'll use to implement the function. We have no choice here, signals are not allowed. Like an entity, "BEGIN" marks the beginning of the body, where the operation of the function is defined, which is fairly obvious—we simply cycle through the array up to the specified "amount" location, replacing the local "temp_max" with any value we find that's larger. Simultaneously we note the location of any larger value as "index", which, when the loop has completed, will contain the location of the largest value that had been found.

Finally, the second "RETURN" specifies the value that will be returned from the function, in this case, the "index" indication.

We use the function in the body of the entity as follows:

```
function_out <= largest_value(function_in, 4);
```

In this example, "function_in" is some array in the design that contains a variety of values, of which we wish to find the largest. We're indicating that we only want to look in the first five (0 through 4) locations of the array. Once this line of code executes, "function_out" (which had to be declared as an integer) will contain that location.

Procedures

Where functions are similar to counterparts of the same name in other programming languages, procedures could perhaps be compared to subroutines. Unlike functions, procedures can have multiple outputs, or even no outputs (or even no inputs). While called functions are placed in code where they are replaced by a single calculated value, procedures are typically called as a stand-alone expression to do potentially many different things, virtually anything in fact that the calling code could do—implement state machines, call other sub-modules, emulate a micro-processor.

The structure of procedures are similar to functions in that they are declared at the beginning of the architecture (or in packages). They include I/O ports (except now the ports could be both inputs and outputs), declared local variables, and a body that implements the operation. In a sense, they are much like locally defined and instantiated entity modules.

There is one quirk (I consider it a quirk) of procedures: they have the ability to change the value of signals of similar names from the calling entity. This could be confusing, and therefore dangerous, if done inadvertently.

Packages

Packages can be thought of as a type of include file. Generally, a package will contain declarations and subprograms (generally functions) that are used in multiple modules, thus avoiding repeating them each place. Each module declares the package to be included via something like this, located above the beginning of the entity declaration (i.e., with the library declarations):

```
use work.pkg.all;
```

where in this case the name of the package is "pkg" (it could have been "frog"), and its file name would be "pkg.vhd".

A word of caution: compilers can be picky about the sequence of occurrence of packages and the modules that include them. You might have to first force a compile of the package before attempting to compile the modules that contain it.

Rest of the Rest

The following is a pot-pourri of remnant information that might be useful in your VHDL endeavors.

RTL: I haven't used this acronym, but you will see it. It stands for "Register Transfer Level," and refers to a description of digital operation (i.e. HDL) that includes registers (and thus, easily extendable to counters, state machines, etc.). One of the primary functions of synthesis software is to translate RTL into gate-level interconnections appropriate for ASIC or FPGA implementation.

"RTL" has become somewhat synonymous generically with HDL languages (verilog and VHDL).

Unconnected component input and output ports: unconnected output ports can be assigned "open" in the instantiating port connection list. Input ports have to be tied somehow. E.g., if a scalar input should be tied low, "0" can be used instead of a signal name.

bit assignments: the values available depend on the type, and thus to some extent the libraries used, but the following are common to most logic types:

'0'—logic 0
'1'—logic 1
'X'—unknown
'Z'—high impedance

Underscores ("_"), often used for convenient visual nibble delineation (e.g., in verilog), are not allowed. You could create your own type sets using package-based functions that allow this, and then your code would be very specific to you, and everybody else will be very annoyed. VHDL provides many opportunities to muddle your design.

type conversions: given these signals,

```
signal test1 : std_logic_vector(3 downto 0);
signal test2 : unsigned(3 downto 0);
signal test3 : integer;
signal test4 : signed(3 downto 0);
signal test5 : bit_vector(3 downto 0);
signal test6 : unsigned(3 downto 0);
signal test7 : std_logic_vector(3 downto 0);
signal test8 : std_logic_vector(3 downto 0);
signal test9 : std_logic_vector(3 downto 0);
```

then these conversions are possible using our standard ieee.std_logic_1164 and ieee.numeric_std libraries

```
test1 <= "1010";
test2 <= unsigned(test1);
test3 <= to_integer(test2);
```

```
test4 <= signed(test2);
test5 <= to_bitvector(test1);
test6 <= to_unsigned(test3, 4);
test7 <= std_logic_vector(test2);
test8 <= std_logic_vector(test4);
test9 <= to_stdlogicvector(test5);
```

Index

Made in the USA
Middletown, DE
17 December 2019